D0266555

# Knits for Children and their Teddies

# Knits for Children and their Teddies

**Fiona McTague**

COLLINS & BROWN

For Lucy and Molly

First published in Great Britain in 2003 by
Collins & Brown Ltd
The Chrysalis Building
Bramley Road
London W10 6SP

An imprint of **Chrysalis** Books Group plc

Project Manager: Nicola Hodgson
Editor: Sue Whiting
Designer: Gemma Wilson
Photographer: Joey Toller

10 9 8 7 6 5 4 3 2 1

British Library Cataloguing-in-Publication Data:
A catalogue record for this title is available from the British Library.

ISBN 1–84340–020–0 (hb)

Reproduced by Classic Scan Pte Ltd, Singapore
Printed by Imago, Singapore

# contents

# *introduction*

After completing a fashion and textile course I realized that it was my dream to work in the knitwear field, as I loved exploring colors and textures.

My mother inspired me to knit my first teddy sweater from scraps of wool many years ago. It was my pride and joy!

There are over twenty projects that will appeal to children and adults alike. These range from simple, easy-to-knit designs for the complete beginner to more ambitious creations for the experienced knitter.

There are some very simple projects a child could knit for his or her favorite teddy, with a little help from an adult. The up-to-date designs include simple sweaters, blankets, a teddy backpack, and a little teddy that is perfect to put in your pocket.

I hope you enjoy knitting and creating these projects as much as I did designing them. Happy Knitting.

# simple sweater

Simple and easy, ideal for the whole family. Knitted in stockinette (stocking) stitch, finished with a double rib and a stockinette (stocking) stitch roll detail.

## Sizes and finished knitted measurements

| | Bear's Sweater | | | Child's Sweater | | | | | |
|---|---|---|---|---|---|---|---|---|---|
| | | | | months | | | years | | |
| To fit size/age | small | medium | large | 0–6 | 6–12 | 1–2 | 3–4 | 4–5 | yrs |
| Chest size | 7$\frac{1}{2}$ | 10 | 13 | 16 | 18 | 22 | 24 | 27 | in |
| | 19 | 25 | 33 | 41 | 46 | 56 | 61 | 69 | cm |
| Actual width | 4$\frac{3}{4}$ | 6$\frac{1}{8}$ | 7$\frac{1}{2}$ | 8$\frac{7}{8}$ | 11 | 12$\frac{1}{2}$ | 14 | 15$\frac{3}{8}$ | in |
| | 12 | 15$\frac{1}{2}$ | 19 | 22$\frac{1}{2}$ | 28 | 32 | 35$\frac{1}{2}$ | 39 | cm |
| Length to shoulder | 3$\frac{1}{2}$ | 4$\frac{3}{4}$ | 6 | 7$\frac{3}{4}$ | 9$\frac{3}{4}$ | 11$\frac{3}{4}$ | 13$\frac{3}{4}$ | 15$\frac{3}{4}$ | in |
| | 9 | 12 | 15 | 20 | 25 | 30 | 35 | 40 | cm |
| Sleeve length | 2$\frac{3}{4}$ | 3$\frac{1}{2}$ | 4$\frac{1}{4}$ | 5 | 6$\frac{1}{2}$ | 7$\frac{3}{4}$ | 8$\frac{1}{2}$ | 9$\frac{1}{2}$ | in |
| | 7 | 9 | 11 | 13 | 17 | 20 | 22 | 24 | cm |

## Materials

**YARN:** 1 (1: 2: 3: 4: 4: 5: 6) x 50g (1$\frac{1}{4}$oz) balls of Jaeger Extra Fine Merino DK in camel, soft blue, pink, cream or grey

**KNITTING NEEDLES:** Pair each of 3$\frac{1}{4}$mm (US size 3/UK No.10) and 4mm (US size 6/UK No.8) needles

**BUTTONS:** 3 for Bear's Sweater

## Abbreviations

See page 93.

## Stitch gauge/tension

22 sts and 30 rows to 4in, 10cm, measured over stockinette (stocking) stitch on 4mm (US size 6/UK No.8) needles.

## Back

With 3$\frac{1}{4}$mm (US size 3/UK No.10) needles, cast on 26 (34: 42: 50: 62: 70: 78: 86) sts.

Starting with a k row, work in stockinette (stocking) stitch for 4 (4: 4: 4: 6: 6: 6: 6) rows, ending with a WS row.

**RIB ROW 1 (RS):** K2, *p2, k2; rep from * to end.

**RIB ROW 2:** P2, *k2, p2; rep from * to end.

These 2 rows form rib.

Work in rib for a further 2 (2: 2: 2: 4: 4: 4: 4) rows, ending with a WS row.

Change to 4mm (US size 6/UK No.8) needles.

Starting with a k row, work in stockinette (stocking) stitch until Back measures 3$\frac{1}{2}$ (4$\frac{3}{4}$: 6: 7$\frac{3}{4}$: 9$\frac{3}{4}$: 11$\frac{3}{4}$: 13$\frac{3}{4}$: 15$\frac{3}{4}$)in, 9 (12: 15: 20: 25: 30: 35: 40)cm, ending with a WS row.

## Shape shoulders

Bind (cast) off 5 (8: 10: 14: 19: 22: 25: 28) sts at beg of next 2 rows.

Leave rem 16 (18: 22: 22: 24: 26: 28: 30) sts on a holder.

## Front

Work as given for Back until Front measures 2$\frac{3}{4}$ (4: 4$\frac{3}{4}$: 6: 7$\frac{3}{4}$: 9$\frac{3}{4}$:

$11^{3}/_{4}$: $13^{3}/_{4}$)in, 7 (10: 12: 15: 20: 25: 30: 35)cm, ending with a WS row.

### Shape neck

**NEXT ROW (RS):** K9 (13: 16: 19: 24: 27: 30: 34) and turn, leaving rem sts on a holder.

Work on this set of sts only for first side of neck.

Dec 1 st at neck edge of next 4 (5: 6: 5: 5: 5: 5: 6) rows. 5 (8: 10: 14: 19: 22: 25: 28) sts.

Cont straight until Front matches Back to start of shoulder shaping, ending with a WS row.

### Shape shoulder

Bind (cast) off rem 5 (8: 10: 14: 19: 22: 25: 28) sts.

With RS facing, slip center 8 (8: 10: 12: 14: 16: 18: 18) sts onto a holder, rejoin yarn to rem sts, k to end.

Complete to match first side, reversing shaping, working an extra row before start of shoulder shaping.

## Sleeves (make 2)

With $3^{1}/_{4}$mm (US size 3/UK No.10) needles, cast on 22 (26: 26: 30: 34: 38: 42: 46) sts.

Starting with a k row, work in stockinette (stocking) stitch for 4 (4: 4: 4: 6: 6: 6: 6) rows, ending with a WS row.

Work in rib as given for Back for 4 (4: 4: 4: 6: 6: 6: 6) rows, inc 1 (0: 1: 1: 0: 0: 0: 0) st at each end of last row and ending with a WS row. 24 (26: 28: 32: 34: 38: 42: 46) sts.

Change to 4mm (US size 6/UK No.8) needles.

Starting with a k row, work in stockinette (stocking) stitch, shaping sides by inc 1 st at each end of $5^{th}$ ($5^{th}$: $3^{rd}$: $5^{th}$: $3^{rd}$: $3^{rd}$: $5^{th}$: $5^{th}$) and every foll $6^{th}$ ($7^{th}$: $5^{th}$: $7^{th}$: $3^{rd}$: $4^{th}$: $5^{th}$: $6^{th}$) row until there are 28 (30: 34: 38: 52: 56: 60: 64) sts.

Cont straight until Sleeve measures $2^{3}/_{4}$ ($3^{1}/_{2}$: $4^{1}/_{4}$: 5: $6^{1}/_{2}$: $7^{3}/_{4}$: $8^{1}/_{2}$: $9^{1}/_{2}$)in, 7 (9: 11: 13: 17: 20: 22: 24)cm, ending with a WS row.
Bind (cast) off.

## Neckband

Join right shoulder seam.

With RS facing and $3^{1}/_{4}$mm (US size 3/UK No.10) needles, pick up and knit 5 (6: 9: 14: 16: 16: 16: 17) sts down left side of neck, knit across 8 (8: 10: 12: 14: 16: 18: 18) sts left on front holder, pick up and knit 5 (6: 9: 14: 16: 16: 16: 17) sts up right side of neck, then knit across 16 (18: 22: 22: 24: 26: 28: 30) sts left on back holder. 34 (38: 50: 62: 70: 74: 78: 82) sts.

Starting with rib row 2, work in rib as given for Back for 3 (3: 3: 7: 9: 9: 9: 9) rows, ending with a WS row.

Starting with a k row, work in stockinette (stocking) stitch for 2 (2: 4: 4: 4: 4: 4: 4) rows, ending with a WS row.
Bind (cast) off.

## Making up

### Bear's sweater

Join left shoulder seam for $^{1}/_{2}$in, 1cm, from armhole edge. Make 3 button loops across left front shoulder edge and attach buttons to back shoulder edge.

### Child's sweater

Join left shoulder to Neckband, reversing seam for roll.

### All sweaters

Matching center of bind-off (cast-off) edge of Sleeves to shoulder seams, sew Sleeves to Back and Front. Join side and sleeve seams, reversing seam for roll at lower edges.

# Fair Isle sweater

A perfect matching outfit for a child and furry friend. This sophisticated Fair Isle sweater can be knitted in a choice of colorway, with either tan or dark blue as the predominant color.

## Sizes and finished knitted measurements

|  | Bear's Sweater | Child's Sweater |  |
| --- | --- | --- | --- |
| To fit size/age | medium | 4–5 years |  |
| Chest size | 13 | 61 | in |
|  | 33 | 24 | cm |
| Actual width | 6$^{1}$/$_{2}$ | 14$^{1}$/$_{8}$ | in |
|  | 16$^{1}$/$_{2}$ | 36 | cm |
| Length to shoulder | 4$^{3}$/$_{4}$ | 14 | in |
|  | 12 | 36 | cm |
| Sleeve length | 2 | 3$^{1}$/$_{2}$ | in |
|  | 5.5 | 9 | cm |

## Materials

**YARN:** 1 (3) × 50g (1$^{3}$/$_{4}$oz) balls of Rowan True 4-ply Botany in A (charcoal or camel), and 1 ball in each of B (cherry or navy), C (lavender), D (cream), E (pink), F (green) and G (turquoise or cherry)
**KNITTING NEEDLES:** Pair each of 2$^{3}$/$_{4}$mm (US size 2/UK No.12) and 3$^{1}$/$_{4}$mm (US size 3/UK No.10) needles
**BUTTONS:** 3

## Abbreviations

See page 93.

## Stitch gauge/tension

31 sts and 35 rows to 4in, 10cm, measured over fairisle pattern, 28 sts and 36 rows to 4in, 10cm, measured over stockinette (stocking) stitch on 3$^{1}$/$_{4}$mm (US size 3/UK No.10) needles.

## Note

When working from charts, work odd numbered rows as knit rows, reading chart from right to left, and even numbered rows as purl rows, reading chart from left to right. Strand yarn not in use loosely across WS of work.

## Back

With 2$^{3}$/$_{4}$mm (US size 2/UK No.12) needles and yarn A, cast on 51 (111) sts.
**RIB ROW 1 (RS):** K1, *p1, k1; rep from * to end.
**RIB ROW 2:** P1, *k1, p1; rep from * to end.
These 2 rows form rib.
Work in rib for a further 6 (8) rows, ending with a WS row.
Change to 3$^{1}$/$_{4}$mm (US size 3/UK No.10) needles.
Starting and ending rows as indicated and repeating the 30-row pattern repeat as required, cont in patt from chart until Back measures 2 (8$^{1}$/$_{4}$)in, 5 (21)cm, ending with a WS row.

### Shape armholes

Keeping patt correct, bind (cast) off 5 (8) sts at beg of next 2 rows. 41 (95) sts.
Dec 0 (1) st at each end of next and foll 0 (3) alt rows. 41 (87) sts.**
Cont straight until armhole measures $^{3}$/$_{4}$ (3$^{1}$/$_{2}$)in, 2 (9)cm, ending with a WS row.

### Divide for back-opening neck

**NEXT ROW (RS):** Patt 19 (41) sts and turn, leaving rem sts on a holder.
Work on this set of sts only for first side.
Cont straight until armhole measures 2$^{3}$/$_{4}$ (6)in, 7 (15)cm, ending with a WS row.

### Shape shoulder

Bind (cast) off 6 (13) sts at beg of next and foll alt row.
Work 1 row.
Leave rem 7 (15) sts on a holder.

With RS facing, slip center 3 (5) sts onto a holder, rejoin appropriate yarn to rem sts, patt to end.

Complete to match first side, reversing shaping, working an extra row before start of shoulder shaping.

## Front

Work as given for Back to **.

Cont straight until armhole measures $1^{1}/_{2}$ $(4^{1}/_{4})$in, 4 (11)cm, ending with a WS row.

### Shape neck

**NEXT ROW (RS):** Patt 15 (32) sts and turn, leaving rem sts on a holder. Work on this set of sts only for first side of neck.

Dec 1 st at neck edge of next and foll 2 (5) alt rows. 12 (26) sts.

Cont straight until Front matches Back to start of shoulder shaping, ending with a WS row.

### Shape shoulder

Bind (cast) off 6 (13) sts at beg of next row.

Work 1 row.

Bind (cast) off rem 6 (13) sts.

With RS facing, slip center 11 (23) sts onto a holder, rejoin appropriate yarn to rem sts, patt to end.

Complete to match first side, reversing shaping, working an extra row before start of shoulder shaping.

## Sleeves (make 2)

With $2^{3}/_{4}$mm (US size 2/UK No.12) needles and yarn A, cast on 41 (61) sts.

Work in rib as given for Back for 4 (6) rows, ending with a WS row.

Change to $3^{1}/_{4}$mm (US size 3/UK No.10) needles.

Starting and ending rows as indicated and repeating the 30-row pattern repeat as required, cont in patt from chart, shaping sides by inc 1 st at each end of 3$^{rd}$ and every foll 0 (alt) row until there are 43 (83) sts.

### Bear's sweater

Cont straight until Sleeve measures $2^{3}/_{4}$in, 7cm, ending with a WS row.

Place markers along row end edges $^{5}/_{8}$in, 1.5cm, down from bind-off (cast-off) edge to mark top of sleeve seam.

### Child's sweater

Work 1 row, ending with a WS row.

### Shape top

Place markers at both ends of last row to mark top of sleeve seam.

Work 10 rows.

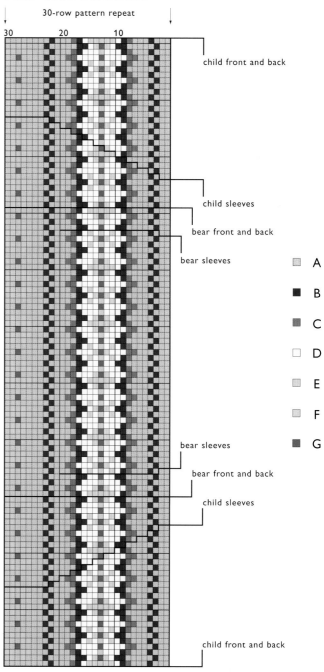

## Fair Isle sweater

30-row pattern repeat

30    20    10

child front and back

child sleeves

bear front and back

bear sleeves

bear sleeves

bear front and back

child sleeves

child front and back

A
B
C
D
E
F
G

Keeping patt correct, dec 1 st at each end of next and foll 3 alt rows.
75 sts.
Work 1 row, ending with a WS row.
**Both sweaters**
Bind (cast) off rem 43 (75) sts.

# Button band

With 2³/₄mm (US size 2/UK No.12) needles and yarn A, cast on
5 (7) sts.
Starting with rib row 1, work in rib as given for Back for 18 (30)
rows, ending with a WS row.
Break yarn and leave sts on a holder.

# Buttonhole band

Slip 3 (5) sts left on holder at base of back opening onto 2³/₄mm
(US size 2/UK No.12) needles and rejoin yarn A with RS facing.
**ROW 1 (RS):** K1, M1, k1 (3), M1, k1. 5 (7) sts.
Starting with rib row 2, work in rib as given for Back for 3 (7) rows,
ending with a WS row.
**NEXT ROW (RS):** Rib 2 (3), yrn, work 2 tog, rib 1 (2).
Work in rib for a further 7 (11) rows.
**NEXT ROW (RS):** Rib 2 (3), yrn, work 2 tog, rib 1 (2).
Work in rib for a further 5 (9) rows, ending with a WS row.
Do NOT break yarn.

# Neckband

Join shoulder seams
With RS facing, 2³/₄mm (US size 2/UK No.12) needles and yarn A,
rib across first 4 (6) sts of Buttonhole Band, k tog last st of
Buttonhole Band with first st left on left back neck holder, knit across
rem 6 (14) sts from holder, pick up and knit 8 (17) sts down left side
of neck, knit across 11 (23) sts left on front holder, pick up and knit 6
(14) sts up right side of neck, knit across first 6 (14) sts left on right
back neck holder, k tog last st of back neck with first st of Button
Band, rib across rem 4 (6) sts of Button Band. 49 (99) sts.
Keeping rib correct as set by Bands, work 1 row, ending with a
WS row.
**NEXT ROW (RS):** Rib 2 (3), yrn, work 2 tog, rib to end.
Work in rib for a further 2 (4) rows.
Bind (cast) off in rib.

# Making up

Matching center of bind-off (cast-off) edge of Sleeves to shoulder
seams, sew Sleeves to Back and Front. Join side and sleeve seams.
Slipstitch bands in place to back opening edges, securing cast-on edge
of Button Band behind Buttonhole Band. Sew on buttons.

# shirt-neck sweater

A crisp, cotton sweater for afternoon teas in the garden.
It looks complex, but it is easy to knit.

## Sizes and finished knitted measurements

| | | Bear's Sweater | | | Child's Sweater | | | | | |
|---|---|---|---|---|---|---|---|---|---|---|
| To fit size/age | S | M | L | XL | 3–4 | 4–5 | 6–7 | 8–9 | 10–11 | yrs |
| Chest size | 8 | 11 | $12^3/4$ | $16^1/2$ | 24 | 25 | 27 | 29 | 31 | in |
| | 20 | 28 | 32 | 42 | 61 | 64 | 69 | 74 | 79 | cm |
| Actual width | $5^1/2$ | $6^1/4$ | $7^1/2$ | $9^1/2$ | 13 | $14^1/2$ | $15^3/8$ | $16^1/4$ | $17^7/8$ | in |
| | 13 | 16 | 19 | 24 | 33 | 37 | 39 | $42^1/2$ | $45^1/2$ | cm |
| Length to shoulder | 4 | $4^3/4$ | $5^1/2$ | $6^1/2$ | $14^1/4$ | $15^3/4$ | $17^1/4$ | 19 | $20^1/2$ | in |
| | 10 | 12 | 14 | 17 | 36 | 40 | 44 | 48 | 52 | cm |
| Sleeve length | 3 | $3^1/2$ | $4^1/4$ | 5 | 9 | $9^3/4$ | 11 | $12^1/4$ | $13^1/4$ | in |
| | 8 | 9 | 11 | 13 | 23 | 25 | 28 | 31 | 34 | cm |

## Materials

**YARN:** 1 (1: 2: 2: 3: 6: 6: 7: 8: 9) x 50g ($1^3/4$oz) balls of Rowan Cotton Glacé in white

**KNITTING NEEDLES:** Pair each of $2^3/4$mm (US size 2/UK No.12) and $3^1/4$mm (US size 3/UK No.10) needles

## Abbreviations

See page 93.

## Stitch gauge/tension

26 sts and 34 rows to 4in, 10cm, measured over stockinette (stocking) stitch on $3^1/4$mm (US size 3/UK No.10) needles.

## Back

With $2^3/4$mm (US size 2/UK No.12) needles, cast on 26 (34: 42: 50: 62: 94: 102: 110: 118) sts.

**RIB ROW 1 (RS):** K2, *p2, k2; rep from * to end.

**RIB ROW 2:** P2, *k2, p2; rep from * to end.

These 2 rows form rib.

Work in rib for a further 6 (6: 12: 12: 12: 16: 16: 16: 16) rows, inc 0 (0: 0: 0: 0: 1: 0: 0: 0) st at each end of last row and ending with a WS row. 26 (34: 42: 50: 62: 96: 102: 110: 118) sts.

Change to $3^1/4$mm (US size 3/UK No.10) needles.

Starting with a k row, work in stockinette (stocking) stitch until Back measures $1^1/2$ (2: $2^1/4$: 3: 4: $10^1/4$: $11^1/2$: $12^1/2$: $13^3/4$)in, 4 (5: 6: 8: 10: 26: 29: 32: 35)cm, ending with a WS row.

### Shape armholes

Bind (cast) off 3 (3: 3: 4: 4: 6: 6: 8: 8) sts at beg of next 2 rows. 20 (28: 36: 42: 54: 82: 90: 94: 102) sts.

Dec 1 st at each end of next 0 (1: 2: 2: 2: 5: 5: 5: 5) rows. 20 (26: 32: 38: 50: 72: 80: 84: 92) sts.**

Cont straight until armhole measures $1^1/2$ (2: $2^1/4$: $2^1/4$: $2^3/4$: $5^1/2$: 5: $6^1/4$: $6^1/2$)in, 4 (5: 6: 6: 7: 14: 15: 16: 17)cm, ending with a WS row.

### Shape shoulders

Bind (cast) off 5 (6: 8: 10: 13: 21: 24: 25: 28) sts at beg of next 2 rows.

Leave rem 10 (14: 16: 18: 24: 30: 32: 34: 36) sts on a holder.

## Front

Work as given for Back to **.

Work 0 (1: 0: 0: 0: 1: 1: 1: 1) row, ending with a WS row.

### Divide for front opening

**NEXT ROW (RS):** K9 (12: 14: 17: 23: 32: 36: 38: 42) and turn, leaving rem sts on a holder.

Work on this set of sts only for first side of neck.

Cont straight until armhole measures $^3/_4$ ($1^1/_4$: $1^1/_4$: $1^1/_4$: $1^1/_2$: 4: $4^1/_4$: $4^3/_4$: 5)in, 2 (3: 3: 3: 4: 10: 11: 12: 13)cm, ending with a RS row.

### Shape neck

Bind (cast) off 1 (3: 3: 4: 5: 5: 6: 6: 7) sts at beg of next row. 8 (9: 11: 13: 18: 27: 30: 32: 35) sts.

Dec 1 st at neck edge of next 3 (3: 3: 3: 5: 6: 6: 7: 7) rows. 5 (6: 8: 10: 13: 21: 24: 25: 28) sts.

Cont straight until Front matches Back to start of shoulder shaping, ending with a WS row.

### Shape shoulder

Bind (cast) off rem 5 (6: 8: 10: 13: 21: 24: 25: 28) sts.

With RS facing, rejoin yarn to rem sts, bind (cast) off center 2 (2: 4: 4: 4: 8: 8: 8: 8) sts, k to end.

Complete to match first side, reversing shaping, working an extra row before start of neck and shoulder shaping.

## Sleeves (make 2)

With $2^3/_4$mm (US size 2/UK No.12) needles, cast on 22 (26: 30: 38: 46: 54: 54: 58: 58) sts.

Work in rib as given for Back for 8 (8: 10: 10: 18: 18: 18: 18: 18) rows, inc 0 (0: 0: 0: 0: 0: 1: 0: 1) st at each end of last row and ending with a WS row. 22 (26: 30: 38: 46: 54: 56: 58: 60) sts.

Change to $3^1/_4$mm (US size 3/UK No.10) needles.

Starting with a k row, work in stockinette (stocking) stitch, shaping sides by inc 1 st at each end of 3rd and every foll alt (alt: alt: alt: alt: 3rd: 4th: 4th: 4th) row until there are 32 (42: 46: 58: 68: 86: 90: 94: 98) sts.

Cont straight until Sleeve measures $2^1/_4$ (3: $3^1/_2$: $4^1/_4$: 5: $9^3/_4$: 11: $12^1/_4$: $13^1/_4$)in, 6 (8: 9: 11: 13: 25: 28: 31: 34)cm, ending with a WS row.

### Shape top

Place markers at both ends of last row to indicate top of sleeve seam.

Work 4 (4: 4: 6: 6: 8: 8: 10: 10) rows, ending with a WS row.

Dec 1 st at each end of next 0 (1: 2: 2: 2: 4: 4: 4: 4) rows.

Bind (cast) off rem 32 (40: 42: 54: 64: 78: 82: 86: 90) sts.

## Front Bands (both alike)

With RS facing and $2^3/_4$mm (US size 2/UK No.12) needles, pick up and knit 6 (6: 10: 10: 14: 26: 30: 34: 38) sts evenly along one side of front opening.

Starting with rib row 2, work in rib as given for Back for 3 (3: 5: 5: 7: 9: 9: 9: 9) rows, ending with a WS row.

Bind (cast) off in rib.

Repeat on opposite side.

## Collar

Join shoulder seams

With RS facing and $2^3/_4$mm (US size 2/UK No.12) needles, starting and ending halfway across top of Front Bands, pick up and knit 8 (8: 11: 12: 13: 22: 23: 26: 29) sts up right side of neck, knit across 10 (14: 16: 18: 24: 30: 32: 34: 36) sts left on back holder, then pick up and knit 8 (8: 11: 12: 13: 22: 23: 26: 29) sts down left side of neck. 26 (30: 38: 42: 50: 74: 78: 86: 94) sts.

Starting with rib row 1, work in rib as given for Back for 14 (14: 18: 18: 20: 28: 28: 28: 28) rows, ending with a WS row.

Bind (cast) off in rib.

## Making up

Matching center of bind-off (cast-off) edge of Sleeves to shoulder seams, sew Sleeves to Back and Front. Join side and sleeve seams.

Lay one Front Band over other and sew to bind (cast) off sts at base of front opening.

# *teddy sweater*

A cuddly sweater with a cuddly motif: a perfect combination of two lovely textures—rustic tweed complemented by velvety chenille.

## Sizes and finished knitted measurements

| | Bear's Sweater | | | Child's Sweater | | | | | |
|---|---|---|---|---|---|---|---|---|---|
| | | | | months | | | years | | |
| To fit size/age | small | medium | large | 0–6 | 6–12 | 2–3 | 4–5 | 6–7 | |
| Chest size | $7^1/2$ | 10 | 13 | 16 | 18 | 22 | 24 | 27 | in |
| | 19 | 25 | 33 | 41 | 46 | 56 | 61 | 69 | cm |
| Actual width | $4^1/2$ | $5^7/8$ | $7^1/2$ | 9 | $11^1/4$ | $12^3/4$ | $14^1/8$ | $15^3/4$ | in |
| | $11^1/2$ | 15 | 19 | 23 | $28^1/2$ | $32^1/2$ | 36 | 40 | cm |
| Length to shoulder | $3^1/2$ | $4^3/4$ | 6 | $7^3/4$ | $9^3/4$ | $11^3/4$ | $13^3/4$ | $15^3/4$ | in |
| | 9 | 12 | 15 | 20 | 25 | 30 | 35 | 40 | cm |
| Sleeve length | $2^3/4$ | $3^1/2$ | $4^1/4$ | 5 | $6^1/2$ | $7^3/4$ | $8^1/2$ | $9^1/2$ | in |
| | 7 | 9 | 11 | 13 | 17 | 20 | 22 | 24 | cm |

## Materials

**YARN:** 1 (1: 2: 3: 4: 4: 5: 5) x 50g ($1^3/4$oz) balls of Rowan Rowanspun DK in A (green or russet)
1 x 50g ($1^3/4$oz) ball of Rowan Fine Cotton Chenille in B (brown)
Scrap of black yarn for embroidery

**KNITTING NEEDLES:** 4mm (US size 6/UK No.8) needles
**BUTTONS:** 2 (2: 2: 2: 3: 3: 3: 3: 3)

## Abbreviations

See page 93.

## Stitch gauge/tension

21 sts and 30 rows to 4in, 10cm, measured over stockinette (stocking) stitch on 4mm (US size 6/UK No.8) needles.

## Note

When working from chart, work odd numbered rows as knit rows, reading chart from right to left, and even numbered rows as purl rows, reading chart from left to right. Use a separate ball of yarn for each block of color, twisting yarns together where they meet to avoid holes forming.

## Back

With 4mm (US size 6/UK No.8) needles and yarn A, cast on 24 (32: 40: 48: 60: 68: 76: 84) sts.

Starting with a k row, work in stockinette (stocking) stitch until Back measures $3^1/_2$ ($4^3/_4$: 6: $7^3/_4$: $9^3/_4$: $11^3/_4$: $13^3/_4$: $15^3/_4$)in, 9 (12: 15: 20: 25: 30: 35: 40)cm, ending with a WS row.

### Shape shoulders

Bind (cast) off 4 (7: 9: 13: 18: 21: 24: 27) sts at beg of next 2 rows.
Leave rem 16 (18: 22: 22: 24: 26: 28: 30) sts on a holder.

## Front

Work as given for Back until Front measures $^3/_4$ ($1^1/_4$: 2: $2^1/_4$: $2^1/_4$: 3: $4^1/_4$: $5^1/_2$)in, 2 (3: 5: 6: 6: 8: 11: 14)cm, ending with a WS row.

**NEXT ROW (RS):** K5 (9: 13: 17: 17: 21: 25: 29), work next 14 (14: 14: 14: 26: 26: 26: 26) sts as row 1 of chart A (A: A: A: B: B: B: B), k to end.

**NEXT ROW:** P5 (9: 13: 17: 17: 21: 25: 29), work next 14 (14: 14: 14: 26: 26: 26: 26) sts as row 2 of chart A (A: A: A: B: B: B: B), p to end.

These 2 rows set position of chart.

Cont as now set until all 12 (12: 12: 12: 38: 38: 38: 38) rows of chart have been completed, ending with a WS row.

Starting with a k row, cont in stockinette (stocking) stitch until Front measures $2^3/_4$ (4: $4^3/_4$: $6^1/_4$: $7^3/_4$: $9^3/_4$: $11^3/_4$: $13^3/_4$)in, 7 (10: 12: 16: 20: 25: 30: 35)cm, ending with a RS row.

### Shape neck

**NEXT ROW (WS):** P8 (12: 15: 18: 23: 26: 29: 33) and turn, leaving rem sts on a holder.

Work on this set of sts only for first side of neck.

Dec 1 st at neck edge of next 4 (5: 6: 5: 5: 5: 5: 5) rows. 4 (7: 9: 13: 18: 21: 24: 27) sts.

Cont straight until Front matches Back to start of shoulder shaping, ending with a RS row.

### Shape shoulder

Bind (cast) off rem 4 (7: 9: 13: 18: 21: 24: 27) sts.

With WS facing, slip center 8 (8: 10: 12: 14: 16: 18: 18) sts onto a holder, rejoin yarn to rem sts, p to end.

Dec 1 st at neck edge of next 4 (5: 6: 5: 5: 5: 5: 5) rows. 4 (7: 9: 13: 18: 21: 24: 27) sts.

Cont straight until Front matches Back to start of shoulder shaping, ending with a WS row.

### Shape shoulder buttonhole band

Work 2 rows, ending with a WS row.

**NEXT ROW (RS):** K1 (3: 4: 2: 5: 6: 7: 8), yfwd, k2tog, (k0 (0: 0: 4: 5: 6:

## child's teddy sweater

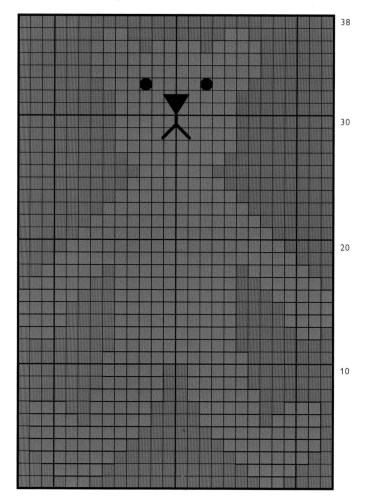

■ A     ■ B

7: 8), yfwd, k2tog) 0 (0: 0: 1: 1: 1: 1: 1) times, k1 (2: 3: 3: 4: 5: 6: 7).
Work 1 row.
Bind (cast) off rem 4 (7: 9: 13: 18: 21: 24: 27) sts.

## Sleeves (make 2)

With 4mm (US size 6/UK No.8) needles and yarn A, cast on 24 (26: 28: 32: 34: 38: 42: 46) sts.
Starting with a k row, work in stockinette (stocking) stitch, shaping

## bear's teddy sweater

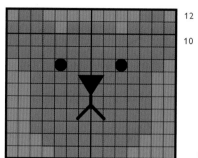

■ A   ■ B

sides by inc 1 st at each end of 5th (7th: 5th: 7th: 3rd: 5th: 5th: 5th)
and every foll 7th (9th: 8th: 9th: 5th: 5th: 6th: 7th) row until there are
28 (30: 34: 38: 52: 56: 60: 64) sts.
Cont straight until Sleeve measures 2³⁄₄ (3¹⁄₂: 4¹⁄₄: 5: 6¹⁄₂: 7³⁄₄: 8¹⁄₂:
9¹⁄₂)in, 7 (9: 11: 13: 17: 20: 22: 24)cm, ending with a WS row.
Bind (cast) off.

## Neckband

Join right shoulder seam.
With RS facing, 4mm (US size 6/UK No.8) needles and yarn A,
pick up and knit 6 (6: 9: 14: 16: 16: 16: 16) sts down left side of neck,
knit across 8 (8: 10: 12: 14: 16: 18: 18) sts left on front holder; pick
up and knit 6 (6: 9: 14: 16: 16: 16: 16) sts up right side of neck, then
knit across 16 (18: 22: 22: 24: 26: 28: 30) sts left on back holder.
36 (38: 50: 62: 70: 74: 78: 80) sts.
**NEXT ROW (WS):** Purl.
**NEXT ROW:** K2, yfwd, k2tog, k to end.
Starting with p row, work in stockinette (stocking) stitch for a
further 3 (3: 3: 5: 5: 5: 5: 5) rows, ending with a WS row.
Bind (cast) off.

## Making up

Overlap left front shoulder edge over back shoulder edge for
4 rows and stitch together at armhole edge. Matching center of
bind-off (cast-off) edge of Sleeves to shoulder seams, sew Sleeves
to Back and Front. Join side and sleeve seams. Sew on buttons.
### Embroidery
Using yarn F and following photograph as a guide, embroider
french knot eyes, satin stitch nose and straight stitch mouth onto
bear motif.

# striped top and pants

This nautically-inspired outfit is perfect for a day out by the sea.

## Sizes and finished knitted measurements

| | Bear | | | Child | | | | | |
|---|---|---|---|---|---|---|---|---|---|
| To fit size/age | small | medium | large | 0–1 | 2–3 | 4–5 | 6–7 | 8–9 | yrs |
| Chest size | 10 | 13 | 16 | 18 | 22 | 24 | 26 | 28 | in |
| | 25 | 33 | 41 | 46 | 56 | 61 | 66 | 71 | cm |
| **Top** | | | | | | | | | |
| Actual width | $6^{1}/_{4}$ | $7^{5}/_{8}$ | $9^{1}/_{2}$ | $10^{3}/_{4}$ | $12^{3}/_{4}$ | $13^{3}/_{4}$ | 15 | $16^{1}/_{2}$ | in |
| | 16 | $19^{1}/_{2}$ | 23 | $27^{1}/_{2}$ | $32^{1}/_{2}$ | 35 | $38^{1}/_{2}$ | 42 | cm |
| Length to shoulder | 4 | 5 | $7^{1}/_{2}$ | $8^{1}/_{2}$ | 10 | $11^{3}/_{4}$ | $13^{3}/_{4}$ | 15 | in |
| | 10 | 13 | 19 | 22 | 26 | 30 | 35 | 39 | cm |
| Sleeve length | $3^{1}/_{2}$ | 4 | 5 | $6^{1}/_{2}$ | $7^{3}/_{4}$ | $8^{1}/_{2}$ | $9^{1}/_{2}$ | 10 | in |
| | 9 | 11 | 13 | 17 | 20 | 22 | 24 | 26 | cm |
| **Trousers** | | | | | | | | | |
| Actual hip measurement | $11^{3}/_{4}$ | 16 | 19 | $22^{3}/_{4}$ | $25^{1}/_{2}$ | 30 | 31 | 33 | in |
| | 30 | 41 | 48 | 58 | 65 | 76 | 79 | 84 | cm |
| Length to waist | 5 | $7^{3}/_{4}$ | $9^{3}/_{4}$ | $13^{3}/_{4}$ | 15 | 17 | 20 | 23 | in |
| | 13 | 20 | 25 | 35 | 39 | 44 | 51 | 59 | cm |
| Inside leg length | 2 | 3 | 4 | 6 | $6^{1}/_{2}$ | $7^{3}/_{4}$ | 9 | $10^{1}/_{2}$ | in |
| | 6 | 8 | 10 | 15 | 17 | 20 | 23 | 27 | cm |

## Materials

### Top

**YARN:** 1 (1: 1: 2: 2: 3: 4: 5) × 50g ($1^{3}/_{4}$oz) balls of Rowan Cotton Glacé in A (purple or white) and 1 (1: 1: 1: 1: 2: 2: 2) balls in B (white or pink)

**KNITTING NEEDLES:** Pair each of $3^{1}/_{4}$mm (US size 3/UK No.10) and $3^{3}/_{4}$ mm (US size 5/UK No.9) needles

**BUTTONS:** 2 (2: 2: 3: 3: 3: 3: 3)

### Pants

**YARN:** 1 (2: 2: 3: 4: 5: 6: 6) × 50g ($1^{3}/_{4}$oz) balls of Rowan Cotton Glacé in purple or pink

**KNITTING NEEDLES:** Pair each of $3^{1}/_{4}$mm (US size 3/UK No.10) and $3^{3}/_{4}$mm (US size 5/UK No.9) needles

**ELASTIC:** Waist length of $3/_{8}$ ($3/_{8}$: $3/_{8}$: $5/_{8}$: $5/_{8}$: $5/_{8}$: $5/_{8}$: $5/_{8}$)in, 1 (1: 1: 1.5: 1.5: 1.5: 1.5: 1.5)cm, wide elastic

## Abbreviations

See page 93.

## Stitch gauge/tension

23 sts and 32 rows to 4in, 10cm, measured over stockinette (stocking) stitch on $3^{3}/_{4}$mm (US size 5/UK No.9) needles.

# *top*
## Back

With 3¼mm (US size 3/UK No.10) needles and yarn A, cast on 37 (45: 53: 63: 75: 81: 89: 97) sts.

**ROW 1 (RS):** K1, *p1, k1; rep from * to end.

**ROW 2:** As row 1.

These 2 rows form seed (moss) st.

Work in seed (moss) st for a further 2 rows, ending with a WS row.

**NEXT ROW (RS):** (K1, p1) 1 (1: 1: 1: 1: 1: 2: 2) times, k to last 2 (2: 2: 2: 2: 2: 4: 4) sts, (p1, k1) 1 (1: 1: 1: 1: 1: 2: 2) times.

**NEXT ROW:** (K1, p1) 1 (1: 1: 1: 1: 1: 2: 2) times, k0 (0: 0: 1: 1: 1: 0: 0), p to last 2 (2: 2: 3: 3: 3: 4: 4) sts, k0 (0: 0: 1: 1: 1: 0: 0), (p1, k1) 1 (1: 1:

1: 1: 1: 2: 2) times.

Rep last 2 rows 1 (1: 1: 2: 2: 3: 3: 3) times more, ending with a WS row.

Change to 3¾mm (US size 5/UK No.9) needles.

Starting with a k row, work in striped stockinette (stocking) stitch as follows:-

Using yarn A, work 4 rows.

Join in yarn B.

Using yarn B, work 2 rows.

Last 6 rows form striped stockinette (stocking) stitch.

Cont in striped stockinette (stocking) stitch until Back measures 4 (5: 7½: 8½: 10¼: 11¾: 13¾: 15¼)in, 10 (13: 19: 22: 26: 30: 35: 39)cm, ending with a WS row.

**Shape shoulders**

Bind (cast) off 8 (11: 14: 18: 23: 25: 28: 31) sts at beg of next 2 rows.

Leave rem 21 (23: 25: 27: 29: 31: 33: 35) sts on a holder.

## Front

Work as given for Back until Front measures 1½ (2¾: 4¾: 6: 7½: 7½: 9: 10¼)in, 4 (7: 12: 15: 19: 19: 23: 26)cm, ending with a WS row.

**Divide for front opening**

**NEXT ROW (RS):** K16 (20: 24: 29: 35: 38: 42: 46) and turn, leaving rem sts on a holder.

Work on this set of sts only for first side of neck.

Cont straight until Front measures 2¾ (3½: 6: 6½: 8¼: 9½: 11½: 12½)in, 7 (9: 15: 17: 21: 24: 29: 32)cm, ending with a WS row.

**Shape neck**

Dec 1 st at front opening edge of next 8 (9: 10: 11: 12: 13: 14: 15) rows. 8 (11: 14: 18: 23: 25: 28: 31) sts.

Cont straight until Front matches Back to start of shoulder shaping, ending with a WS row.

**Shape shoulder**

Bind (cast) off rem 8 (11: 14: 18: 23: 25: 28: 31) sts.

With RS facing, slip center 5 sts onto a holder, rejoin yarn to rem sts, k to end.

Complete to match first side, reversing shaping, working an extra row before start of shoulder shaping.

## Sleeves (make 2)

With 3¼mm (US size 3/UK No.10) needles and yarn A, cast on 25 (27: 31: 35: 39: 43: 47: 51) sts.

Work in seed (moss) st as given for Back for 4 rows, ending with a WS row.

Change to 3³/₄mm (US size 5/UK No.9) needles.
Starting with a k row and 4 rows using yarn A, work in striped stockinette (stocking) stitch as given for Back, shaping sides by inc 1 st at each end of 5th and every foll 6th (6th: 6th: 8th: 6th: 6th: 6th: 6th) row until there are 29 (33: 37: 43: 57: 61: 67: 71) sts.
Cont straight until Sleeve measures 3¹/₂ (4¹/₄: 5: 6¹/₂: 7³/₄: 8¹/₂: 9¹/₂: 10¹/₄)in, 9 (11: 13: 17: 20: 22: 24: 26)cm, ending with a WS row.
Bind (cast) off.

### Button band

With 3¹/₄mm (US size 3/UK No.10) needles and yarn A, cast on 5 sts.
Work in seed (moss) st as given for Back until Button Band, when slightly stretched, fits up left side of front opening to neck shaping, sewing in place as you go along and ending with a WS row.
Break yarn and leave sts on a holder.
Mark positions for 2 (2: 2: 3: 3: 3: 3: 3) buttons on this band – top button to come ³/₈in, 1cm, above neck shaping, lowest button to come ³/₈in, 1cm, up from base of front opening and rem 0 (0: 0: 1: 1: 1: 1: 1) button midway between.

### Buttonhole band

Slip 5 sts left on holder at base of front opening onto 3¹/₄mm (US size 3/UK No.10) needles and rejoin yarn A with RS facing.
Work in seed (moss) st as given for Back until Buttonhole Band, when slightly stretched, fits up right side of front opening to neck shaping, sewing in place as you go along, ending with a WS row and with the addition of 1 (1: 1: 2: 2: 2: 2: 2) buttonhole to correspond with positions marked for buttons worked as follows:
**BUTTONHOLE ROW (RS):** K1, p2tog, yrn, p1, k1.
When Buttonhole Band is complete, do NOT break off yarn.

## Neckband

Join shoulder seams.
With RS facing, 3¹/₄mm (US size 3/UK No.10) needles and yarn A, patt across 5 sts of Buttonhole Band, pick up and knit 7 (7: 12: 12: 15: 15: 18: 18) sts up right side of neck, knit across 21 (23: 25: 27: 29: 31: 33: 35) sts left on back holder, pick up and knit 7 (7: 12: 12: 15: 15: 18: 18) sts down left side of neck, then patt across 5 sts of Button Band. 45 (47: 59: 61: 69: 71: 79: 81) sts.
Work in seed (moss) st as set by Bands for 1 (1: 1: 3: 3: 3: 3: 3) rows, ending with a WS row.
**NEXT ROW (RS):** K1, p2tog, yrn, (to make buttonhole) patt to end.
Work in seed (moss) st for a further 3 rows.
Bind (cast) off in patt.

## Making up

Matching center of bind-off (cast-off) edge of Sleeves to shoulder seams, sew Sleeves to Back and Front. Join side and sleeve seams, leaving side seams open for first 8 (8: 8: 10: 10: 12: 12: 12) rows.
Sew cast-on edge of Button Band in place behind Buttonhole Band.
Sew on buttons.

# *pants*

## Legs (make 2)

With 3¹/₄mm (US size 3/UK No.10) needles, cast on 35 (43: 51: 63: 73: 87: 91: 95) sts.
**ROW 1 (RS):** K1, *p1, k1; rep from * to end.
**ROW 2:** As row 1.
These 2 rows form seed (moss) st.
Work in seed (moss) st for a further 0 (0: 0: 2: 2: 2: 2: 2) rows, ending with a WS row.
Change to 3³/₄mm (US size 5/UK No.9) needles.
Starting with a k row, work in stockinette (stocking) stitch, shaping sides by inc 1 st at each end of next and every foll alt (alt: alt: 4th: 4th: 6th: 6th: 6th) row until there are 43 (55: 65: 79: 89: 101: 105: 111) sts.
Cont straight until Leg measures 2¹/₄ (3: 4: 6: 6¹/₂: 7³/₄: 9: 10¹/₂)in, 6 (8: 10: 15: 17: 20: 23: 27)cm, ending with a WS row.

### Shape crotch

Bind (cast) off 2 (2: 2: 3: 3: 3: 3: 3) sts at beg of next 2 rows. 39 (51: 61: 73: 83: 95: 99: 105) sts.
Dec 1 st at each end of next 2 (2: 3: 3: 4: 4: 4: 4) rows. 35 (47: 55: 67: 75: 87: 91: 97) sts.
Cont straight until crotch measures 2³/₄ (4³/₄: 6: 7³/₄: 8¹/₂: 9¹/₂: 11: 12¹/₂)in, 7 (12: 15: 20: 22: 24: 28: 32)cm, ending with a WS row.
**NEXT ROW (RS):** K4 (4: 2: 5: 3: 2: 4: 2), *k2tog, k10 (10: 6: 9: 8: 8: 8: 8); rep from * to last 7 (7: 5: 7: 6: 5: 7: 5) sts, k2tog, k to end. 32 (43: 48: 61: 68: 78: 82: 87) sts.
Work a further 3 (3: 3: 5: 5: 5: 5: 5) rows, ending with a WS row.
Bind (cast) off.

## Making up

Join inside leg seams. Join crotch seam. Join ends of elastic to form a loop and attach to inside of waist edge by working herringbone stitch over the elastic.

# scandinavian sweater

This roomy sweater is great to snuggle into on a chilly day.
The snowflake pattern is worked using the intarsia method.

## Sizes and finished knitted measurements

|  | Bear's Sweater | | | Child's Sweater | | | |
|---|---|---|---|---|---|---|---|
| To fit size/age | small | medium | large | 3–5 | 6–8 | 9–11 | yrs |
| Chest size | 16 | 18 | 22 | 24 | 27 | 31 | in |
|  | 41 | 46 | 56 | 61 | 69 | 78 | cm |
| Actual width | 9 | $11^1/_4$ | $12^3/_4$ | $14^1/_8$ | $15^1/_2$ | $16^7/_8$ | in |
|  | 23 | $28^1/_2$ | $32^1/_2$ | 36 | $39^1/_2$ | 43 | cm |
| Length to shoulder | $8^1/_2$ | $9^3/_4$ | $11^3/_4$ | $13^3/_4$ | $15^3/_4$ | $17^1/_4$ | in |
|  | 22 | 25 | 30 | 35 | 40 | 44 | cm |
| Sleeve length | 5 | $6^1/_2$ | $7^3/_4$ | $8^1/_2$ | $9^1/_2$ | 11 | in |
|  | 13 | 17 | 20 | 22 | 24 | 28 | cm |

## Materials

**YARN:** 2 (3: 4: 5: 6: 7) x 50g ($1^3/_4$oz) balls of Jaeger Extra Fine
Merino DK in A (grey or red), and 1 ball in each of B (red or grey)
and C (cream)
**KNITTING NEEDLES:** Pair each of $3^1/_4$mm (US size 3/UK No.10) and
4mm (US size 6/UK No.8) needles

## Abbreviations

See page 93.

## Stitch gauge/tension

22 sts and 30 rows to 4in, 10cm, measured over stockinette
(stocking) stitch on 4mm (US size 6/UK No.8) needles.

## Note

When working from chart, work odd numbered rows as knit rows,
reading chart from right to left, and even numbered rows as purl
rows, reading chart from left to right. Strand yarn not in use
loosely across WS of work.

## Back

With $3^1/_4$mm (US size 3/UK No.10) needles and yarn A, cast on
50 (62: 70: 78: 86: 94) sts.
**RIB ROW 1 (RS):** K2, *p2, k2; rep from * to end.
**RIB ROW 2:** P2, *k2, p2; rep from * to end.
These 2 rows form rib.
Work in rib for a further 8 (8: 10: 10: 10: 10) rows, inc 1 st at end of
last row and ending with a WS row. 51 (63: 71: 79: 87: 95) sts.
Change to 4mm (US size 6/UK No.8) needles.**
Starting with a k row, work in stockinette (stocking) stitch until Back
measures $8^1/_2$ ($9^3/_4$: $11^3/_4$: $13^3/_4$: $15^3/_4$: $17^1/_4$)in, 22 (25: 30: 35: 40:
44)cm, ending with a WS row.

## Shape shoulders

Bind (cast) off 11 (15: 17: 20: 23: 26) sts at beg of next 2 rows.
Leave rem 29 (33: 37: 39: 41: 43) sts on a holder.

# Front

Work as given for Back to **.

Starting with a k row, work in stockinette (stocking) stitch for 2 (6: 8: 12: 16: 20) rows, ending with a WS row.

***Join in yarn B.

**NEXT ROW (RS):** Using yarn A k3, *using yarn B k1, using yarn A k3; rep from * to end.

**NEXT ROW:** Using yarn B p1, *using yarn A p1, using yarn B p3; rep from * to last 2 sts, using yarn A p1, using yarn B p1.

**NEXT ROW:** Using yarn B k3, *using yarn A k1, using yarn B k3; rep from * to end.

**NEXT ROW:** Using yarn A p1, *using yarn B p1, using yarn A p3; rep from * to last 2 sts, using yarn B p1, using yarn A p1.

Break off yarn B and cont using yarn A only.***

Work 2 rows, ending with a WS row.

Join in yarn C.

## scandinavian sweater

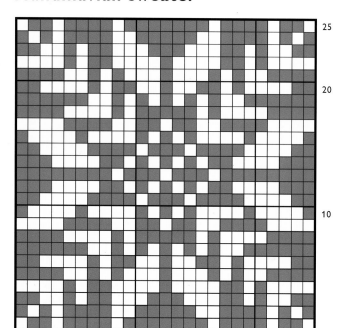

25

20

10

☐ A

▨ B

**NEXT ROW (RS):** K13 (19: 23: 27: 31: 35), work next 25 sts as row 1 of Snowflake Chart, k to end.

**NEXT ROW:** P13 (19: 23: 27: 31: 35), work next 25 sts as row 2 of Snowflake Chart, p to end.

Cont as set until all 25 rows of Snowflake Chart have been completed, ending with a RS row.

Break off yarn C and cont using yarn A only.

Work 2 rows, ending with a RS row.

Join in yarn B.

**NEXT ROW (WS):** Using yarn A p3, *using yarn B p1, using yarn A p3; rep from * to end.

**NEXT ROW:** Using yarn B k1, *using yarn A k1, using yarn B k3; rep from * to last 2 sts, using yarn A k1, using yarn B k1.

**NEXT ROW:** Using yarn B p3, *using yarn A p1, using yarn B p3; rep from * to end.

**NEXT ROW:** Using yarn A k1, *using yarn B k1, using yarn A k3; rep from * to last 2 sts, using yarn B k1, using yarn A k1.

Break off yarn B and cont using yarn A only.

Cont straight until Front measures 6½ (7½: 9½: 11½: 13¼: 15)in, 17 (19: 24: 29: 34: 38)cm, ending with a WS row.

**Shape neck**

**NEXT ROW (RS):** K20 (25: 28: 31: 32: 35) and turn, leaving rem sts on a holder.

Work on this set of sts only for first side of neck.

Dec 1 st at neck edge of next 9 (10: 11: 11: 9: 9) rows. 11 (15: 17: 20: 23: 26) sts.

Cont straight until Front matches Back to start of shoulder shaping, ending with a WS row.

**Shape shoulder**

Bind (cast) off rem 11 (15: 17: 20: 23: 26) sts.

With RS facing, slip center 11 (13: 15: 17: 23: 25) sts onto a holder, rejoin yarn to rem sts, k to end.

Complete to match first side, reversing shaping, working an extra row before start of shoulder shaping.

# Sleeves (make 2)

With 3¼mm (US size 3/UK No.10) needles and yarn A, cast on 34 (38: 42: 46: 50: 54) sts.

Work in rib as given for Back for 10 (10: 12: 12: 12: 12) rows, inc 1 st at end of last row and ending with a WS row. 35 (39: 43: 47: 51: 55) sts.

Change to 4mm (US size 6/UK No.8) needles.

Starting with a k row, work in stockinette (stocking) stitch for 2 rows, ending with a WS row.

Work as given for Front from \*\*\* to \*\*\*.

Cont in stockinette (stocking) stitch, shaping sides by inc 1 st at each end of next and every foll 3rd (3rd: 5th: 4th: 5th: 6th) row until there are 41 (53: 57: 65: 69: 73) sts.

Cont straight until Sleeve measures 5 (6$^1$/$_2$: 7$^3$/$_4$: 8$^1$/$_2$: 9$^1$/$_2$: 11)in, 13 (17: 20: 22: 24: 28)cm, ending with a WS row.

Bind (cast) off.

## Neckband

Join right shoulder seam.

With RS facing, 3$^1$/$_4$mm (US size 3/UK No.10) needles and yarn A, pick up and knit 13 (16: 17: 19: 19: 19) sts down left side of neck, knit across 11 (13: 15: 17: 23: 25) sts left on front holder, pick up and knit 13 (16: 17: 19: 19: 19) sts up right side of neck, then knit across 29 (33: 37: 39: 41: 43) sts left on back holder. 66 (78: 86: 94: 102: 106) sts.

Starting with rib row 2, work in rib as given for Back for 9 (11: 11: 15: 15: 15) rows.

Change to 4mm (US size 6/UK No.8) needles.

Cont in rib for a further 10 (12: 12: 16: 16: 16) rows.

Bind (cast) off in rib.

## Making up

Join left shoulder to Neckband, reversing seam for turn-back.

Matching center of bind-off (cast-off) edge of Sleeves to shoulder seams, sew Sleeves to Back and Front. Join side and sleeve seams.

# *ribbed hooded jacket*

Funky, chunky and bold—perfect for a free-spirited child.
Knitted in a light Aran-weight yarn that can be worn the whole year round.

## Sizes and finished knitted measurements

| | Child | | | | |
|---|---|---|---|---|---|
| To fit age | 1–2 | 2–3 | 4–5 | 6–7 | yrs |
| Chest size | 22 | 24 | 26 | 28 | in |
| | 56 | 61 | 66 | 71 | cm |
| Actual width | $14^1/_8$ | $15^3/_4$ | $17^1/_4$ | $18^3/_4$ | in |
| | 36 | 40 | 44 | $47^1/_2$ | cm |
| Length to shoulder | $12^1/_2$ | $14^1/_2$ | 16 | $17^3/_4$ | in |
| | 32 | 37 | 41 | 45 | cm |
| Sleeve length | 9 | $10^1/_2$ | $12^1/_4$ | $13^3/_4$ | in |
| | 23 | 27 | 31 | 35 | cm |

## Materials

**YARN:** 7 (8: 9: 9) × 50g ($1^3/_4$oz) balls of Rowan All-Seasons Cotton in blue

**KNITTING NEEDLES:** Pair each of 4mm (US size 6/UK No.8) and 5mm (US size 8/UK No.6) needles

**BUTTONS:** 5

## Abbreviations

See page 93.

## Stitch gauge/tension

21 sts and 25 rows to 4in, 10cm, measured over rib on 5mm (US size 8/UK No.6) needles.

## Back

With 4mm (US size 6/UK No.8) needles, cast on 76 (84: 92: 100) sts.

**RIB ROW 1 (RS):** P1, k2, *p2, k2; rep from * to last st, p1.

**RIB ROW 2:** K1, p2, *k2, p2; rep from * to last st, p1.

These 2 rows form rib.

Work in rib for a further 4 rows, ending with a WS row.

Change to 5mm (US size 8/UK No.6) needles.

Cont in rib until Back measures 7 ($8^1/_2$: $9^3/_4$: 11)in, 18 (22: 25: 28)cm, ending with a WS row.

### Shape armholes

Keeping rib correct, bind (cast) off 3 sts at beg of next 2 rows.

70 (78: 86: 94) sts.

Dec 1 st at each end of next 5 rows, then on foll 4 (5: 4: 5) alt rows.

52 (58: 68: 74) sts.

Cont straight until armhole measures $5^1/_2$ (6: $6^1/_4$: $6^1/_2$)in, 14 (15: 16: 17)cm, ending with a WS row.

### Shape shoulders

Bind (cast) off 6 (7: 9: 10) sts at beg of next 2 rows, then 7 (8: 10: 11) sts at beg of foll 2 rows.

Bind (cast) off rem 26 (28: 30: 32) sts.

## Pocket Linings (make 2)

With 5mm (US size 8/UK No.6) needles, cast on 20 sts.

Work in rib as given for Back for 20 rows, ending with a WS row.

Break yarn and leave sts on a holder.

## Left Front

With 4mm (US size 6/UK No.8) needles, cast on 36 (40: 44: 48) sts.

Work in rib as given for Back for 6 rows, ending with a WS row.

Change to 5mm (US size 8/UK No.6) needles.

Cont in rib for a further 20 rows, ending with a WS row.

### Place pocket

**NEXT ROW (RS):** Rib 4 (8: 12: 16), slip next 20 sts onto a holder and, in their place, rib across 20 sts of first Pocket Lining, rib 12.

Cont straight until Left Front matches Back to start of armhole shaping, ending with a WS row.

**Shape armhole**

Keeping rib correct, bind (cast) off 3 sts at beg of next row. 33 (37: 41: 45) sts.

Work 1 row.

Dec 1 st at armhole edge of next 5 rows, then on foll 4 (5: 4: 5) alt rows. 24 (27: 32: 35) sts.

Cont straight until 11 (11: 13: 13) rows fewer have been worked than on Back to start of shoulder shaping, ending with a RS row.

**Shape neck**

Keeping rib correct, bind (cast) off 5 (5: 5: 6) sts at beg of next row. 19 (22: 27: 29) sts.

Dec 1 st at neck edge of next 5 rows, then on foll 1 (2: 3: 3) alt rows. 13 (15: 19: 21) sts.

Work 3 (1: 1: 1) rows, ending with a WS row.

**Shape shoulder**

Bind (cast) off 6 (7: 9: 10) sts at beg of next row.

Work 1 row.
Bind (cast) off rem 7 (8: 10: 11) sts.

## Right Front

Work to match Left Front, reversing shaping, working an extra row before start of armhole, neck and shoulder shaping and placing Pocket as follows:

### Place Pocket

**NEXT ROW (RS):** Rib 12, slip next 20 sts onto a holder and, in their place, rib across 20 sts of second Pocket Lining, rib 4 (8: 12: 16).

## Sleeves (make 2)

With 4mm (US size 6/UK No.8) needles, cast on 36 (36: 40: 40) sts.
Work in rib as given for Back for 6 rows, ending with a WS row.
Change to 5mm (US size 8/UK No.6) needles.
Cont in rib, shaping sides by inc 1 st at each end of 3rd and every foll 3rd (3rd: 4th: 4th) row until there are 66 (70: 74: 78) sts, taking inc sts into rib.
Cont straight until Sleeve measures 10$\frac{1}{2}$ (12$\frac{1}{4}$: 13$\frac{3}{4}$: 15$\frac{1}{4}$)in, 27 (31: 35: 39)cm, ending with a WS row.

### Shape top

Bind (cast) off 3 sts at beg of next 10 (6: 4: 2) rows, then 4 sts at beg of foll 4 (8: 10: 12) rows.
Bind (cast) off rem 20 (20: 22: 24) sts.

## Hood

With 4mm (US size 6/UK No.8) needles, cast on 130 (134: 138: 142) sts.
**RIB ROW 1 (RS):** P0 (2: 0: 2), k2, *p2, k2; rep from * to last 0 (2: 0: 2) sts, p0 (2: 0: 2).
**RIB ROW 2:** K0 (2: 0: 2), p2, *k2, p2; rep from * to last 0 (2: 0: 2) sts, k0 (2: 0: 2).
These 2 rows form rib.
Work in rib for a further 4 rows, ending with a WS row.
Change to 5mm (US size 8/UK No.6) needles.
Cont in rib, dec 1 st at each end of next and foll 9 alt rows.
110 (114: 118: 122) sts.
Cont straight until Hood measures 6 (6$\frac{1}{4}$: 6$\frac{1}{2}$: 7)in, 15 (16: 17: 18)cm, ending with a WS row.

### Shape back

Place marker between center sts of last row.
**NEXT ROW (RS):** Rib to within 3 sts of marker, k2tog, p2 (marker is between these sts), k2tog tbl, rib to end.

**NEXT ROW:** Rib to within 2 sts of marker, p1, k2 (marker is between these sts), p1, rib to end.
Rep last 2 rows twice more. 104 (108: 112: 116) sts.
**NEXT ROW (RS):** Rib to within 3 sts of marker, k2tog, p2 (marker is between these sts), k2tog tbl, rib to end.
**NEXT ROW:** Rib to within 3 sts of marker, p2tog tbl, k2 (marker is between these sts), p2tog, rib to end.
Rep last 2 rows 3 times more.
Bind (cast) off rem 88 (92: 96: 100) sts in rib.

## Button band

With RS facing and 4mm (US size 6/UK No.8) needles, pick up and knit 50 (58: 66: 74) sts evenly along one front opening edge (left front for a girl, or right front for a boy), between cast-on edge and neck shaping.
**RIB ROW 1 (WS):** P2, *k2, p2; rep from * to end.
**RIB ROW 2:** K2, *p2, k2; rep from * to end.
These 2 rows form rib.
Work in rib for a further 3 rows.
Bind (cast) off in rib.

## Buttonhole band

Work to match Button Band with the addition of 5 buttonholes worked in row 2 as follows:
**ROW 2 (RS):** Rib 3, yrn, work 2 tog, *rib 9 (11: 13: 15), yrn, work 2 tog; rep from * to last st, rib 1.

## Pocket borders (both alike)

Slip 20 sts left on Pocket holder onto 4mm (US size 6/UK No.8) needles and rejoin yarn with RS facing.
Work in rib as set for 12 rows.
Bind (cast) off in rib.

## Making up

Sew back seam of Hood. Fold 1$\frac{1}{4}$in, 3cm, to RS along cast-on edge of Hood. Positioning this fold halfway across top of Bands, sew shaped edge of Hood to neck edge, easing in fullness. Join shoulder seams. Matching center of bind-off (cast-off) edge of Sleeves to shoulder seams, sew Sleeves to Back and Fronts. Join side and sleeve seams, reversing sleeve seam for first 2in, 5cm. Fold 1$\frac{1}{2}$in, 4cm, cuff to RS. Fold Pocket Border in half to RS. Sew Pocket Linings in place on inside, then sew down ends of Pocket Borders. Sew on buttons.

# bear's ribbed pullover vest

## Sizes and finished knitted measurements

| | | Bear | | | | |
|---|---|---|---|---|---|---|
| To fit size | XS | S | M | L | XL | |
| Chest size | 13 | 16 | 18 | 20 | 22 | in |
| | 33 | 41 | 46 | 51 | 56 | cm |
| Actual width | $6^1/2$ | $7^7/8$ | $8^1/2$ | $9^1/2$ | $10^3/8$ | in |
| | $16^1/2$ | 20 | $12^1/2$ | 25 | $26^1/2$ | cm |
| Length to shoulder | $4^3/4$ | 5 | $5^1/2$ | 6 | $6^1/4$ | in |
| | 12 | 13 | 14 | 15 | 16 | cm |

## Materials

**YARN:** 1 x 50g ($1^3/4$oz) ball of Rowan All-Seasons Cotton in each of A (blue), B (plum) and C (coral)

**KNITTING NEEDLES:** Pair of 4mm (US size 6/UK No.8) needles

## Abbreviations

See page 93.

## Stitch gauge/tension

24 sts and 26 rows to 4in, 10cm, measured over rib on 4mm (US size 6/UK No.8) needles.

## Back and Front (both alike)

With 4mm (US size 6/UK No.8) needles and yarn A, cast on 40 (48: 52: 60: 64) sts.

**RIB ROW 1 (RS):** P1, k2, *p2, k2; rep from * to last st, p1.

**RIB ROW 2:** K1, p2, *k2, p2; rep from * to last st, p1.

These 2 rows form rib.

Work in rib for a further 2 rows.

Join in yarn B.

Using yarn B, work 4 rows.

Join in yarn C.

Using yarn C, work 4 rows.

Last 12 rows form striped rib.

Cont in striped rib until work measures 2 ($2^1/4$: $2^3/4$: 3)in, 5 (6: 7: 8)cm, ending with a WS row.

## Shape armholes

Keeping rib correct, bind (cast) off 4 sts at beg of next 2 rows. 32 (40: 44: 52: 56) sts.

Dec 1 st at each end of next 4 rows. 24 (32: 36: 44: 48) sts.

Cont straight until armhole measures $1^1/2$ ($1^1/2$: $1^1/2$: $1^1/4$: $1^1/4$)in, 4 (4: 4: 3: 3)cm, ending with a WS row.

## Shape neck

**NEXT ROW (RS):** Rib 8 (11: 11: 13: 13) and turn, leaving rem sts on a holder.

Work on this set of sts only for first side of neck.

Cont straight until armhole measures $2^3/4$in, 7cm, ending with a WS row.

## Shape shoulder

Bind (cast) off rem 8 (11: 11: 13: 13) sts.

With RS facing, rejoin appropriate yarn to rem sts, bind (cast) off center 8 (10: 14: 18: 22) sts, rib to end.

Complete to match first side.

# Making up

Join shoulder seams. Join side seams.

# bear-hooded top and scarf

These cheerful, loveable knits are bound to turn heads. They are easy and enjoyable to knit for all ages, made in gorgeous tweed yarn to make them feel special.

## Sizes and finished knitted measurements

| | Child | | | |
|---|---|---|---|---|
| To fit age | 2–3 | 4–5 | 6–7 | yrs |
| Chest size | 22 | 24 | 26 | in |
| | 56 | 61 | 66 | cm |
| Actual width | 12$^1$/$_2$ | 14 | 15$^3$/$_8$ | in |
| | 32 | 35$^1$/$_2$ | 39 | cm |
| Length to shoulder | 13$^1$/$_4$ | 15$^1$/$_4$ | 17 | in |
| | 34 | 39 | 43 | cm |
| Sleeve length | 9$^3$/$_4$ | 11$^1$/$_2$ | 13 | in |
| | 25 | 29 | 33 | cm |

## Materials

**YARN:** 4 (4: 5) x 50g (1$^3$/$_4$oz) balls of Jaeger Luxury Tweed in A (light brown marl) and oddment in B (beige marl)

**KNITTING NEEDLES:** Pair each of 3$^1$/$_4$mm (US size 3/UK No.10) and 4mm (US size 6/UK No.8) needles

## Abbreviations

See page 93.

## Stitch gauge/tension

23 sts and 31 rows to 4in, 10cm, measured over stockinette (stocking) stitch on 4mm (US size 6/UK No.8) needles.

## Back

With 3$^1$/$_4$mm (US size 3/UK No.10) needles and yarn A, cast on 74 (82: 90) sts.

**RIB ROW 1 (RS):** K2, *p2, k2; rep from * to end.

**RIB ROW 2:** P2, *k2, p2; rep from * to end.

These 2 rows form rib.

Work in rib for a further 12 rows, ending with a WS row.

Change to 4mm (US size 6/UK No.8) needles.

Starting with a k row, work in stockinette (stocking) stitch until Back measures 13$^1$/$_4$ (15$^1$/$_4$: 17)in, 34 (39: 43)cm, ending with a WS row.

### Shape shoulders

Bind (cast) off 12 (14: 15) sts at beg of next 2 rows, then 13 (14: 16) sts at beg of foll 2 rows.

Leave rem 24 (26: 28) sts on a holder.

## Front

Work as given for Back until Front measures 11 (13: 14$^1$/$_2$)in, 28 (33: 37)cm, ending with a WS row.

### Shape neck

**NEXT ROW (RS):** K31 (34: 37) and turn, leaving rem sts on a holder.

Work on this set of sts only for first side of neck.

Dec 1 st at neck edge of next 6 rows. 25 (28: 31) sts.

Cont straight until Front matches Back to start of shoulder shaping, ending with a WS row.

### Shape shoulder

Bind (cast) off 12 (14: 15) sts at beg of next row.

Work 1 row.

Bind (cast) off rem 13 (14: 16) sts.

With RS facing, rejoin yarn to rem sts, bind (cast) off center 12 (14: 16) sts, k to end.

Complete to match first side, reversing shaping, working an extra row before start of shoulder shaping.

## Sleeves (make 2)

With 3$^1$/4mm (US size 3/UK No.10) needles and yarn A, cast on 42 (42: 46) sts.

Work in rib as given for Back for 11 rows, ending with a RS row.

**NEXT ROW (WS):** Rib 3 (3: 1), inc in next st, *rib 6 (4: 5), inc in next st; rep from * to last 3 (3: 2) sts, rib to end. 48 (50: 54) sts.

Change to 4mm (US size 6/UK No.8) needles.

Starting with a k row, work in stockinette (stocking) stitch, shaping sides by inc 1 st at each end of 5$^{th}$ and every foll 6$^{th}$ row until there are 66 (72: 78) sts.

Cont straight until Sleeve measures 9$^3$/4 (11$^1$/2: 13)in, 25 (29: 33)cm, ending with a WS row.

Bind (cast) off.

## Hood

With 4mm (US size 6/UK No.8) needles and yarn A, cast on 20 (24: 26) sts, with RS facing knit across 24 (26: 28) sts left on back holder, turn and cast on 20 (24: 26) sts. 64 (74: 80) sts.

**NEXT ROW (WS):** P3 (8: 1), inc in next st, *p2 (2: 3), inc in next st; rep from * to last 3 (8: 2) sts, p to end. 84 (94: 100) sts.

Starting with a k row, work in stockinette (stocking) stitch until Hood measures 7 (7$^1$/2: 7$^3$/4)in, 18 (19: 20)cm, ending with a WS row.

**Shape top**

Bind (cast) off 31 (35: 37) sts at beg of next 2 rows. 22 (24: 26) sts.

Cont straight until Hood measures 5 (6: 6$^1$/4)in, 13 (15: 16)cm, from bound-off (cast-off) sts, ending with a WS row.

Bind (cast) off.

## Hood Border

Join top hood seams.

With RS facing, 3$^1$/4mm (US size 3/UK No.10) needles and yarn A, pick up and knit 92 (96: 100) sts along front edge of Hood.

**RIB ROW 1 (WS):** P1, k2, *p2, k2; rep from * to last st, p1.

**RIB ROW 2:** K1, p2, *k2, p2; rep from * to last st, k1.

These 2 rows form rib.

Work in rib for a further 6 rows, ending with a RS row.

Bind (cast) off in rib.

## Pocket

With 3$^1$/4mm (US size 3/UK No.10) needles and yarn A, cast on 32 (36: 40) sts.

Starting with rib row 2, work in rib as given for Hood Border for 8 rows, ending with a WS row.

Change to 4mm (US size 6/UK No.8) needles.

Starting with a k row, work in stockinette (stocking) stitch until Pocket measures 6$^1$/4 (6$^1$/2: 7)in, 16 (17: 18)cm, ending with a WS row.

Change to 3$^1$/4mm (US size 3/UK No.10) needles.

Starting with rib row 2, work in rib as given for Hood Border for 8 rows, ending with a WS row.

Bind (cast) off in rib.

## Ears (make 4)

With 4mm (US size 6/UK No.8) needles and yarn A, cast on 16 sts.

Starting with a k row, work in stockinette (stocking) stitch for 14 rows, ending with a WS row.

**ROW 15 (RS):** K3tog, k10, k3tog.

**ROW 16:** P3tog, p6, p3tog.

Bind (cast) off rem 8 sts.

Make other Ear parts in this way—one more using yarn A (these two form outer ears) and two using yarn B (these form inner ears).

## Making up

Join shoulder seams. Sew Hood to neck edge, easing in fullness and with bound (cast) off edges of Hood Border meeting at center front. Matching center of bind-off (cast-off) edge of Sleeves to shoulder seams, sew Sleeves to Back and Front. Join side and sleeve seams. Using photograph as a guide, sew Pocket onto Front. RS facing, sew pairs of inner and outer Ears together, leaving cast-on edge open. Turn RS out and sew to top of Hood as in photograph.

# *bear's scarf*

## Sizes and finished knitted measurements

|  | Bear | | | |
|---|---|---|---|---|
| Actual measurement | $2^3/_8$ | × | $15^3/_8$ | in |
|  | 12 | × | 78 | cm |

## Materials

**YARN:** 1 × 50g ($1^3/_4$oz) ball of Jaeger Luxury Tweed in each of A (beige marl) and B (pink)

**KNITTING NEEDLES:** Pair of 4mm (US size 6/UK No.8) needles

## Abbreviations

See page 93.

## Stitch gauge/tension

23 sts and 31 rows to 4in, 10cm, measured over stockinette (stocking) stitch on 4mm (US size 6/UK No.8) needles.

## Scarf

With 4mm (US size 6/UK No.8) needles and yarn A, cast on 27 sts.

**ROW 1 (RS):** Knit.

**ROW 2:** K2, p23, k2.

Rep these 2 rows until Scarf measures $30^3/_4$ in, 78cm, ending with a WS row.

Bind (cast) off.

## Pockets (make 2)

With 4mm (US size 6/UK No.8) needles and yarn A, cast on 21 sts.

Work in garter stitch for 3 rows, ending with a WS row.

**ROW 1 (RS):** Knit.

**ROW 2:** K2, p17, k2.

**ROWS 3 TO 6:** As rows 1 and 2, twice.

Join in yarn B.

Using a separate ball of yarn for each block of color and twisting yarns together where they meet to avoid holes forming, cont as follows:

**ROW 7:** Using yarn A k10, using yarn B k1, using yarn A k10.

**ROW 8:** Using yarn A k2, p7, using yarn B p3, using yarn A p7, k2.

**ROW 9:** Using yarn A k8, using yarn B k5, using yarn A k8.

**ROW 10:** Using yarn A k2, p5, using yarn B p7, using yarn A p5, k2.

**ROW 11:** Using yarn A k6, using yarn B k9, using yarn A k6.

**ROW 12:** Using yarn A k2, p3, using yarn B p11, using yarn A p3, k2.

**ROW 13:** Using yarn A k4, using yarn B k13, using yarn A k4.

**ROW 14:** Using yarn A k2, p1, using yarn B p15, using yarn A p1, k2.

**ROW 15:** Using yarn A k3, using yarn B k15, using yarn A k3.

**ROWS 16 AND 17:** As rows 14 and 15.

**ROW 18:** Using yarn A k2, p1, (using yarn B p7, using yarn A p1) twice, k2.

**ROW 19:** Using yarn A k4, using yarn B k5, using yarn A k3, using yarn B k5, using yarn A k4.

**ROW 20:** Using yarn A k2, p3, using yarn B p3, using yarn A p5, using yarn B p3, using yarn A p3, k2.

Break off yarn B and cont using yarn A only.

**ROWS 21 TO 26:** As rows 1 and 2, 3 times.

Work in garter stitch for 3 rows.

Bind (cast) off knitwise (on WS).

## Making up

Sew Pockets onto ends of Scarf. Using yarn B, make 4 pompons, each $1^1/_4$in, 3cm, in diameter and attach to corners of Scarf.

# snowflake jacket

This jacket is perfect for that special someone at Christmas time.
Knit it in poster blue and white, or in shades of cream for a cool and fresh look.

## Sizes and finished knitted measurements

| | Child | | | |
|---|---|---|---|---|
| | months | years | | |
| To fit age | 6–12 | 1–2 | 2–3 | |
| Chest size | 20 | 22 | 24 | in |
| | 41 | 46 | 51 | cm |
| Actual width | 12$^3$/$_8$ | 13 | 14$^1$/$_8$ | in |
| | 31$^1$/$_2$ | 33 | 36 | cm |
| Length to shoulder | 11 | 12$^1$/$_2$ | 13 | in |
| | 28 | 32 | 33 | cm |
| Sleeve length | 7 | 8$^1$/$_4$ | 9 | in |
| | 18 | 21 | 23 | cm |

## Materials

**YARN:** 4 (4: 5) x 50g (1$^3$/$_4$oz) balls of Rowan Wool Cotton in A (blue) and 1 ball in B (cream)

**KNITTING NEEDLES:** Pair each of 3$^1$/$_4$mm (US size 3/UK No.10) and 4mm (US size 6/UK No.8) needles

**BUTTONS:** 5

## Abbreviations

See page 93.

## Stitch gauge/tension

22 sts and 30 rows to 4in, 10cm, measured over stockinette (stocking) stitch on 4mm (US size 6/UK No.8) needles.

## Note

When working from charts, work odd numbered rows as knit rows, reading chart from right to left, and even numbered rows as purl rows, reading chart from left to right. Use a separate ball of yarn for each snowflake, weaving yarns together around snowflake. Do NOT work partial snowflake motifs.

## Back

With 3$^1$/$_4$mm (US size 3/UK No.10) needles and yarn A, cast on 69 (73: 79) sts.

**ROW 1 (RS):** K1, *p1, k1; rep from * to end.

**ROW 2:** As row 1.

These 2 rows form seed (moss) st.

Work in seed (moss) st for a further 8 rows, ending with a WS row.

Change to 4mm (US size 6/UK No.8) needles.

Starting and ending rows as indicated, now work in patt from chart for Back and Fronts until chart row 74 (86: 90) has been completed, ending with a WS row.

### Shape shoulders

Bind (cast) off 10 (11: 12) sts at beg of next 2 rows, then 11 (11: 12) sts at beg of foll 2 rows.

Leave rem 27 (29: 31) sts on a holder.

## Left Front

With 3$^1$/$_4$mm (US size 3/UK No.10) needles and yarn A, cast on 33 (35: 37) sts.

Work in seed (moss) st as given for Back for 10 rows, inc 0 (0: 1) st at end of last row and ending with a WS row. 33 (35: 38) sts.

Change to 4mm (US size 6/UK No.8) needles.

Starting and ending rows as indicated, now work in patt from chart for Back and Fronts until chart row 61 (73: 77) has been completed, ending with a RS row.

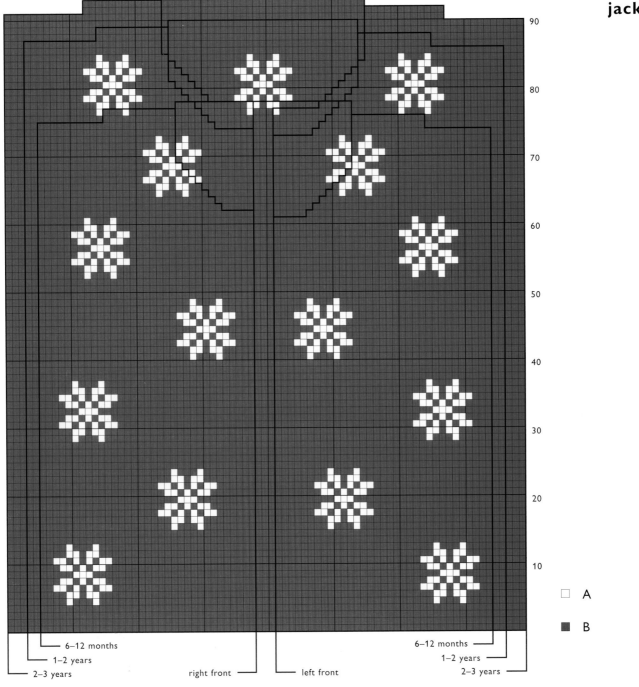

90

80

70

60

50

40

30

20

10

□ A

■ B

6–12 months
1–2 years
2–3 years
right front
left front
6–12 months
1–2 years
2–3 years

## Shape neck

Keeping chart correct, bind (cast) off
5 (6: 7) sts at beg of next row.
28 (29: 31) sts.
Dec 1 st at neck edge of next 7 rows.
21 (22: 24) sts.
Work 5 rows, completing chart row
74 (86: 90) and ending with a WS row.

## Shape shoulder

Bind (cast) off 10 (11: 12) sts at beg of
next row.
Work 1 row.
Bind (cast) off rem 11 (11: 12) sts.

# Right Front

Work to match Left Front, reversing shaping,
working an extra row before start of neck and
shoulder shaping.

# Sleeves (make 2)

With 3¹/₄mm (US size 3/UK No.10) needles and
yarn A, cast on 35 (37: 39) sts.
Work in seed (moss) st as given for Back for 10
rows, ending with a WS row.
Change to 4mm (US size 6/UK No.8) needles.
Starting and ending rows as indicated, now work in
patt from chart for Sleeves, shaping sides by inc 1 st
at each end of 5ᵗʰ and every foll 4ᵗʰ row until there
are 55 (59: 65) sts.
Cont straight until chart row 44 (52: 60) has been
completed, ending with a WS row.
Bind (cast) off.

**sleeve**

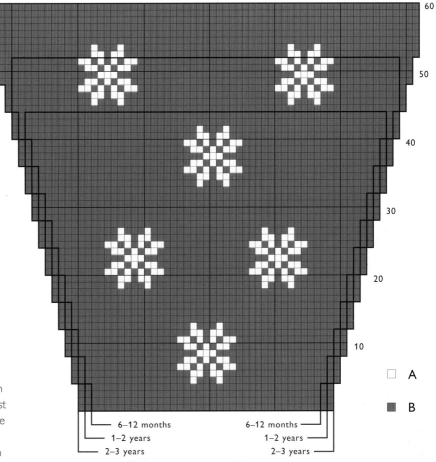

# Button band

With 3¹/₄mm (US size 3/UK No.10) needles and yarn A,
cast on 7 sts.
Work in seed (moss) st as given for Back until Button Band, when
slightly stretched, fits up left front opening edge to neck shaping,
sewing in place as you go along and ending with a WS row.
Bind (cast) off.
Mark positions for 5 buttons on the Button Band—first and last
buttons to be ¹/₂in, 1.2cm, from ends of band and rem 3 buttons
evenly spaced between.

# Buttonhole band

Work to match Button Band with the addition of 5 buttonholes to
correspond with positions marked for buttons worked as follows:-
**BUTTONHOLE ROW (RS):** K1, p1, k2tog, yfwd, k1, p1, k1.

# Collar

Join shoulder seams
With RS facing, 3¹/₄mm (US size 3/UK No.10) needles and yarn A,
starting and ending halfway across top of Bands, pick up and knit
20 (22: 23) sts up right side of neck, knit across 27 (29: 31) sts left

on Back holder inc 2 sts, then pick up and knit 20 (22: 23) sts down left side of neck. 69 (75: 79) sts.

**ROW 1:** K3, *p1, k1; rep from * to last 2 sts, k2.

**ROW 2:** As row 1.

These 2 rows set position of seed (moss) st with first and last 2 sts of every row worked as knit sts.

Keeping sts correct, cont as follows:

**ROW 3:** K2, patt to last 3 sts, inc twice in next st, k2.

Rep row 3 until Collar measures 2³/4in, 7cm.

Bind (cast) off in patt.

## Making up

Matching center of bound-off (cast-off) edge of Sleeves to shoulder seams, sew Sleeves to Back and Fronts. Join side and sleeve seams. Sew on buttons.

# *snowflake hat and scarf*

### Sizes and finished knitted measurements

|  | Bear |  |
|---|---|---|
| Hat |  |  |
| Width around head | 13³/4 | in |
|  | 35 | cm |
| Scarf |  |  |
| Width | 3 | in |
|  | 8 | cm |
| Length (excluding fringe) | 24 | in |
|  | 61 | cm |

### Materials

**YARN:** 1 x 50g (1³/4oz) ball of Rowan Wool Cotton in each of A (blue) and B (cream)

**KNITTING NEEDLES:** Pair each of 3¹/4mm (US size 3/UK No.10) and 4mm (US size 6/UK No.8) needles

### Abbreviations

See page 93.

### Stitch gauge/tension

22 sts and 30 rows to 4in, 10cm, measured over stockinette (stocking) stitch on 4mm (US size 6/UK No.8) needles.

## hat

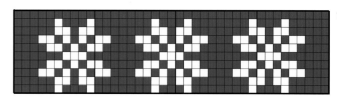

## scarf

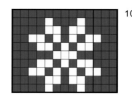

☐ A

■ B

# Hat

With 3¹/4mm (US size 3/UK No.10) needles and yarn A, cast on 39 sts.

**ROW 1 (RS):** K1, *p1, k1; rep from * to end.

**ROW 2:** As row 1.

These 2 rows form seed (moss) st.

Work in seed (moss) st for a further 8 rows, ending with a WS row. Change to 4mm (US size 6/UK No.8) needles.

Starting with a k row, work in stockinette (stocking) stitch for 4 rows, ending with a WS row.

Now work in patt from chart for Hat until chart row 10 has been completed, ending with a WS row.

Starting with a k row, work in stockinette (stocking) stitch for a further 18 rows, ending with a WS row.

Bind (cast) off.

Make a second piece in exactly the same way.

Join pieces together, leaving cast-on edges open. Using yarn A, make two twisted cords, each 2¹/2in, 6cm, long, and two tassels, each 1¹/2in, 4cm, long. Attach a tassel to one end of each cord and then attach other ends of cords to corners of Hat.

## Scarf

With 3¼mm (US size 3/UK No.10) needles and yarn A, cast on 17 sts.

Work in seed (moss) st as given for Hat for 6 rows, ending with a WS row.

Change to 4mm (US size 6/UK No.8) needles.

**ROW 1 (RS):** Knit.

**ROW 2:** K2, p13, k2.

These 2 rows set position of stockinette (stocking) st with first and last 2 sts of every row worked as knit sts.

Keeping sts correct, cont as follows:

Work 2 rows.

**\*\*NEXT ROW (RS):** K2, work next 13 sts as row 1 of Scarf Chart, k2.

**NEXT ROW:** K2, work next 13 sts as row 2 of Scarf Chart, k2.

Cont as set until all 10 rows of chart have been completed.\*\*

Cont using yarn A only until Scarf measures 21¼in, 54cm, ending with a WS row.

Rep from \*\* to \*\* once more.

Cont using yarn A only for a further 4 rows, ending with a WS row.

Change to 3¼mm (US size 3/UK No.10) needles.

Work in seed (moss) st as given for Hat for 6 rows, ending with a WS row.

Bind (cast) off.

Cut 4in, 10cm, lengths of yarn A and knot groups of 5 of these lengths through both ends of Scarf to form fringe, making 6 knots evenly spaced across each end. Trim fringe.

# Aran coat and hat

Keep the frost outside and stay toasty warm in this chunky coat and hat. This big and easy-to-knit outfit has been made in natural shades, but don't be afraid to go brighter.

## Sizes and finished knitted measurements

|  | Bear | | Child | | |
|---|---|---|---|---|---|
| To fit size/age | medium | 4–5 | 6–7 | 8–9 | yrs |
| Chest size | 12 | 24 | 26 | 28 | in |
|  | 31 | 61 | 66 | 71 | cm |
| Actual width | 8¼ | 16⅛ | 17⅛ | 17⅞ | in |
|  | 21 | 41 | 43½ | 45½ | cm |
| Length to shoulder | 8¼ | 17 | 18 | 19¼ | in |
|  | 21 | 43 | 46 | 49 | cm |
| Sleeve length | 4 | 9½ | 10½ | 12¼ | in |
|  | 10 | 24 | 27 | 31 | cm |

## Materials

**YARN:** 2 (5: 6: 7) x 100g (3½oz) balls of Rowan Magpie Aran in dark camel or gray

**KNITTING NEEDLES:** Pair each of 3¾mm (US size 5/UK No.9) and 4½mm (US size 7/UK No.7) needles

**BUTTONS:** 6 (8: 8: 8)

## Abbreviations

See page 93.

## Stitch gauge/tension

18 sts and 26 rows to 4in, 10cm, measured over stockinette (stocking) stitch on 4½mm (US size 7/UK No.7) needles.

# coat
## Back

With 3¾mm (US size 5/UK No.9) needles, cast on 38 (74: 78: 82) sts.

**RIB ROW 1 (RS):** K2, *p2, k2; rep from * to end.

**RIB ROW 2:** P2, *k2, p2; rep from * to end.

These 2 rows form rib.

Work in rib for a further 4 (6: 6: 6) rows, ending with a WS row.

Change to 4½mm (US size 7/UK No.7) needles.

Starting with a k row, now work in stockinette (stocking) stitch until Back measures 8¼ (17: 18: 19¼)in, 21 (43: 46: 49)cm, ending with a WS row.

### Shape shoulders

Bind (cast) off 6 (12: 13: 14) sts at beg of next 4 rows.

Bind (cast) off rem 14 (26: 26: 26) sts.

## Left Front

With 3¾mm (US size 5/UK No.9) needles, cast on 19 (35: 39: 39) sts.

**RIB ROW 1 (RS):** *K2, p2; rep from * to last 3 sts, k3.

**RIB ROW 2:** K1, p2, *k2, p2; rep from * to end.

These 2 rows form rib.

Work in rib for a further 4 (6: 6: 6) rows, inc 1 (2: 0: 2) sts evenly across last row and ending with a WS row. 20 (37: 39: 41) sts.

Change to 4½mm (US size 7/UK No.7) needles.

Starting with a k row, now work in stockinette (stocking) stitch until Left Front measures 7 (15: 16: 17¼)in, 18 (38: 41: 44)cm, ending with a RS row.

### Shape neck

Bind (cast) off 4 (7: 7: 7) sts at beg of next row. 16 (30: 32: 34) sts.

Dec 1 st at neck edge of next 4 rows, then on foll 0 (2: 2: 2) alt rows. 12 (24: 26: 28) sts.

Cont straight until Left Front matches Back to start of shoulder shaping, ending with a WS row.

## Shape shoulder

Bind (cast) off 6 (12: 13: 14) sts at beg of next row.

Work 1 row.

Bind (cast) off rem 6 (12: 13: 14) sts.

## Right Front

With 3³/₄mm (US size 5/UK No.9) needles, cast on 19 (35: 39: 39) sts.

**RIB ROW 1 (RS):** K3, *p2, k2; rep from * to end.

**RIB ROW 2:** *P2, k2; rep from * to last 3 sts, p2, k1.

These 2 rows form rib.

Complete to match Left Front, reversing shapings, working an extra row before start of neck and shoulder shaping.

## Sleeves (make 2)

With 3³/₄mm (US size 5/UK No.9) needles, cast on 26 (34: 34: 38) sts.

Work in rib as given for Back for 9 (15: 15: 15) rows, ending with a RS row.

**NEXT ROW (WS):** Rib 6 (3: 1: 3), inc in next st, *rib 12 (8: 5: 5), inc in next st; rep from * to last 6 (3: 2: 4) sts, rib to end. 28 (38: 40: 44) sts.

Change to 4¹/₂mm (US size 7/UK No.7) needles.

Starting with a k row, now work in stockinette (stocking) stitch, shaping sides by inc 1 st at each end of 5th (3rd: 3rd: 5th) and every foll 5th (4th: 5th: 6th) row until there are 34 (62: 64: 66) sts.

Cont straight until Sleeve measures 5 (11: 12¹/₄: 14)in, 13 (28: 31: 36)cm, ending with a WS row.

Bind (cast) off.

## Pockets (make 2)

With 4¹/₂mm (US size 7/UK No.7) needles, cast on 12 (20: 20: 20) sts.

Starting with a k row, work in stockinette (stocking) stitch for 14 (26: 26: 26) rows, inc 1 st at each end of last row and ending with a WS row. 14 (22: 22: 22) sts.

Change to 3³/₄mm (US size 5/UK No.9) needles.

Starting with rib row 2, work in rib as given for Back for 8 (12: 12: 12) rows, ending with a WS row.

Bind (cast) off in rib.

## Buttonhole band

With RS facing and 3³/₄mm (US size 5/UK No.9) needles, pick up and knit 46 (78: 86: 94) sts evenly along one front opening edge (left front for a boy, or right front for a girl), between cast-on edge and neck shaping.

Starting with rib row 2, work in rib as given for Back for 1 (3: 3: 3) rows, ending with a WS row.

**NEXT ROW (RS):** Rib 3 (3: 2: 3), *bind (cast) off 2 sts, rib until there are 11 (12: 14: 15) sts on right needle after bind-off (cast-off); rep from * to last 4 (5: 4: 6) sts, bind (cast) off 2 sts, rib to end.

**NEXT ROW:** Rib to end, casting on 2 sts over those bound (cast) off on previous row.

Work in rib for a further 2 rows.

Bind (cast) off in rib.

## Button band

With RS facing and 3³/₄mm (US size 5/UK No.9) needles, pick up and knit 46 (78: 86: 94) sts evenly along one front opening edge (right front for a boy, or left front for a girl), between cast-on edge and neck shaping.

Starting with rib row 2, work in rib as given for Back for 5 (7: 7: 7) rows, ending with a WS row.

Bind (cast) off in rib.

## Collar

Join shoulder seams.

With RS facing and 3³/₄mm (US size 5/UK No.9) needles, starting and ending halfway across top of Bands, pick up and knit 17 (25: 25: 25) sts up right side of neck, 20 (36: 36: 36) sts across back neck, and 17 (25: 25: 25) sts down left side of neck. 54 (86: 86: 86) sts.

Starting with rib row 2, work in rib as given for Back for 2¹/₄ (3¹/₂: 3¹/₂: 3¹/₂)in, 6 (9: 9: 9)cm.

Bind (cast) off loosely in rib.

## Making up

Matching center of bound-off (cast-off) edge of Sleeves to shoulder seams, sew Sleeves to Back and Fronts. Join side and sleeve seams, reversing sleeve seam for first 1¹/₄ (1¹/₂: 1¹/₂: 2)in, 3 (4: 4: 5)cm, for turn-back cuff. Fold cuff to RS. Fold ribbed section of Pocket onto RS and then sew Pockets to Fronts as in photograph. Secure ribbed section in place by centrally attaching a button. Sew on buttons.

## *hat*

With 3³/₄mm (US size 5/UK No.9) needles, cast on 86 (90: 94: 98) sts.

Work in rib as given for Back of Coat for 3¹/₂ (5¹/₂: 6¹/₄: 7)in, 9 (14: 16: 18)cm, ending with rib row 2.

**Shape crown**

**ROW 1 (RS):** K2, *p2tog, k2; rep from * to end. 65 (68: 71: 74) sts.

**ROW 2:** P2, *k1, p2; rep from * to end.

**ROW 3:** K2, *p1, k2; rep from * to end.

**ROW 4:** As row 2.

**ROW 5:** K2tog, *p1, k2tog; rep from * to end. 43 (45: 47: 49) sts.

**ROW 6:** P1, *k1, p1; rep from * to end.

**ROW 7:** K1, (k2tog) to end. 22 (23: 24: 25) sts.

**ROW 8:** P0 (1: 0: 1), (p2tog) to end.

Break yarn and thread through rem 11 (12: 12: 13) sts. Pull up tight and fasten off securely. Join back seam, reversing seam for first 1¹/₂in, 4cm, for turn-back. Fold turn-back to RS.

# *zipped jacket*

This easy-to-knit zip-up jacket can be customized in your favorite colors. Knit teddy a hat and scarf too, and the wearers will be sure to turn heads.

## Sizes and finished knitted measurements

| | Child | | | |
|---|---|---|---|---|
| To fit age | 1–2 | 2–3 | 4–5 | yrs |
| Chest size | 22 | 24 | 26 | in |
| | 46 | 51 | 56 | cm |
| Actual width | 12$^{1}/_{4}$ | 13$^{1}/_{4}$ | 14$^{1}/_{8}$ | in |
| | 31 | 33$^{1}/_{2}$ | 36 | cm |
| Length | 11$^{3}/_{4}$ | 14 | 15$^{3}/_{4}$ | in |
| | 30 | 36 | 40 | cm |
| Sleeve length | 7 | 7$^{3}/_{4}$ | 9$^{3}/_{4}$ | in |
| | 18 | 20 | 25 | cm |

## Materials

**YARN:** 2 (2: 3) x 50g (1$^{3}/_{4}$oz) balls of Rowan Wool Cotton in A (dark lilac), 3 (3: 4) balls in B (rose pink), 1 (1: 2) balls in C (denim blue) and oddment in D (turquoise) for embroidery

**KNITTING NEEDLES:** Pair each of 3$^{1}/_{4}$mm (US size 3/UK No.10) and 3$^{3}/_{4}$mm (US size 5/UK No.9) needles

**ZIP:** Open-ended zip to fit

## Abbreviations

See page 93.

## Stitch gauge/tension

24 sts and 32 rows to 4in, 10cm, measured over stockinette (stocking) stitch on 3$^{3}/_{4}$mm (US size 5/UK No.9) needles.

## Back

With 3$^{3}/_{4}$mm (US size 5/UK No.9) needles and yarn A, cast on 74 (80: 86) sts.

Starting with a k row, work in stockinette (stocking) stitch until Back measures 6$^{1}/_{2}$ (8$^{1}/_{2}$: 9$^{3}/_{4}$)in, 17 (22: 25)cm, ending with a WS row.

## Shape raglan armholes

Bind (cast) off 2 sts at beg of next 2 rows. 70 (76: 82) sts.

**NEXT ROW (RS):** K2, p2, k2tog, k to last 6 sts, sl 1, k1, psso, p2, k2.

**NEXT ROW:** Purl.

Rep last 2 rows 19 (21: 22) times more.

Leave rem 30 (32: 36) sts on a holder.

## Left Front

With 3$^{3}/_{4}$mm (US size 5/UK No.9) needles and yarn B, cast on 38 (41: 44) sts.

Starting with a k row, work in stockinette (stocking) stitch until Left Front matches Back to start of raglan armhole shaping, ending with a WS row.

## Shape raglan armhole

Bind (cast) off 2 sts at beg of next row. 36 (39: 42) sts.

Work 1 row.

**NEXT ROW (RS):** K2, p2, k2tog, k to end.

**NEXT ROW:** Purl.

Rep last 2 rows 9 (11: 10) times more. 26 (27: 31) sts.

## Shape neck

**NEXT ROW (RS):** K2, p2, k2tog, k11 (11: 15) and turn, leaving rem 9 (10: 10) sts on a holder. 16 (16: 20) sts.

**NEXT ROW:** Purl.

Working all raglan decreases as set, dec 1 st at each end of next and foll 4 (4: 6) alt rows. 6 sts.

Work 1 row.

**NEXT ROW (RS):** K2, p1, p3tog.

**NEXT ROW:** P4.

**NEXT ROW:** K1, sl1, k2tog, psso.

**NEXT ROW:** P2.

**NEXT ROW:** K2tog and fasten off.

## Right Front

With 3³/₄mm (US size 5/UK No.9) needles and yarn B, cast on 38 (41: 44) sts.

Starting with a k row, work in stockinette (stocking) stitch until Right Front matches Back to start of raglan armhole shaping, ending with a RS row.

### Shape raglan armhole

Bind (cast) off 2 sts at beg of next row. 36 (39: 42) sts.

**NEXT ROW (RS):** K to last 6 sts, sl 1, k1, psso, p2, k2.

**NEXT ROW:** Purl.

Rep last 2 rows 9 (11: 10) times more. 26 (27: 31) sts.

### Shape neck

**NEXT ROW (RS):** K9 (10: 10) and slip these sts onto a holder, k11 (11: 15), sl 1, k1, psso, p2, k2. 16 (16: 20) sts.

**NEXT ROW:** Purl.

Working all raglan decreases as set, dec 1 st at each end of next and foll 4 (4: 6) alt rows. 6 sts.

Work 1 row.

**NEXT ROW (RS):** P3tog, p1, k2.

**NEXT ROW:** P4.

**NEXT ROW:** K3tog, k1.

**NEXT ROW:** P2.

**NEXT ROW:** K2tog and fasten off.

## Left Sleeve

With 3³/₄mm (US size 5/UK No.9) needles and yarn C, cast on 34 (38: 42) sts.

Starting with a k row, work in stockinette (stocking) stitch, shaping sides by inc 1 st at each end of 7th and every foll 4th (4th: 5th) row until there are 54 (62: 66) sts.

Cont straight until Sleeve measures 7 (7³/₄: 9³/₄)in, 18 (20: 25)cm, ending with a WS row.

### Shape raglan

Bind (cast) off 2 sts at beg of next 2 rows. 50 (58: 62) sts.

### 2nd and 3rd sizes only

**NEXT ROW (RS):** K2, p2, k2tog, k to last 6 sts, sl 1, k1, psso, p2, k2.

**NEXT ROW:** P4, p2tog tbl, p to last 6 sts, p2tog, p4.

Rep last 2 row (1: 2) times more. 50 sts.

### All sizes

**NEXT ROW (RS):** K2, p2, k2tog, k to last 6 sts, sl 1, k1, psso, p2, k2.

**NEXT ROW:** Purl.**

Rep last 2 rows 17 times more. 14 sts.

**NEXT ROW (RS):** K2, p2, k2tog, k4 and turn.

**NEXT ROW:** P9.

**NEXT ROW:** K2, p2, k2tog, k1 and turn.

**NEXT ROW:** P6.

Break yarn and leave rem 12 sts on a holder.

## Right Sleeve

Work as given for Left Sleeve to **.

Rep last 2 rows 16 times more and then first of these rows again. 14 sts.

**NEXT ROW (WS):** P10 and turn.

**NEXT ROW:** K4, sl 1, k1, psso, p2, k2.

**NEXT ROW:** P7 and turn.

**NEXT ROW:** K1, sl 1, k1, psso, p2, k2.

**NEXT ROW:** P6.

Break yarn and leave rem 12 sts on a holder.

## Collar

Join raglan seams

With RS facing, 3¹/₄ mm (US size 3/UK No.10) needles and yarn A, knit across 9 (10: 10) sts from right front neck holder, pick up and knit 16 (16: 20) sts up right side of neck, knit across 12 sts left on right sleeve holder as follows: (k1, k2tog) 4 times, 30 (32: 36) sts left on back holder dec 4 sts evenly, and 12 sts left on left sleeve holder as follows: (k2tog, k1) 4 times, pick up and knit 16 (16: 20) sts down left side of neck, then knit across 9 (10: 10) sts from left front neck holder. 92 (96: 108) sts.

**ROW 1:** Knit.

**ROW 2:** K2, p to last 2 sts, k2.

Rep last 2 rows until Collar measures 3¹/₄in, 8cm, ending with row 1.

Knit 2 rows.

Bind (cast) off knitwise.

## Making up

Join side and sleeve seams. Using yarn D, work blanket stitch around all edges. Insert zip into front opening.

# bear's hat and scarf

## Sizes and finished knitted measurements

|  | Bear | | | |
|---|---|---|---|---|
| To fit size | small | medium | large | |
| **Hat** | | | | |
| Width around head | 11³/₄ | 12¹/₂ | 13¹/₄ | in |
|  | 30 | 32 | 34 | cm |
| **Scarf** | | | | |
| Width | 3 | 4 | 6¹/₂ | in |
|  | 8 | 10 | 17 | cm |
| Length | 30³/₄ | 35¹/₂ | 40 | in |
|  | 78 | 90 | 102 | cm |

## Materials

**YARN:** 1 × 50g (1³/₄oz) ball of Rowan Wool Cotton in each of A (denim blue), B (turquoise) and C (navy)

**KNITTING NEEDLES:** Pair each of 3¹/₄mm (US size 3/UK No.10) and 3³/₄mm (US size 5/UK No.9) needles

## Abbreviations

See page 93.

## Stitch gauge/tension

32 sts and 28 rows to 4in, 10cm, measured over rib on 3³/₄ mm (US size 5/UK No.9) needles.

# Hat

With 3¹/₄mm (US size 3/UK No.10) needles and yarn A, cast on 97 (103: 109) sts.

**ROW 1 (RS):** K1, *p1, k1; rep from * to end.

**ROW 2:** P1, *k1, p1; rep from * to end.

These 2 rows form rib.

Work in rib for a further 4 rows, ending with a WS row.

Change to 3³/₄mm (US size 5/UK No.9) needles.

Cont in rib until Hat measures 3¹/₂ (4¹/₄: 5¹/₂)in, 9, (11: 14)cm, ending with a WS row.

## Shape crown

**ROW 1 (RS):** K1, p1, *sl 1, k2tog, psso, p1, k1, p1; rep from * to last 5 sts, k3tog, p1, k1. 65 (69: 73) sts.

Work 3 rows.

**ROW 5:** K1, *p1, sl 1, k2tog, psso; rep from * to end. 33 (35: 37) sts.

**ROW 6:** (P2tog) to last st, p1.

Break yarn and thread through rem 17 (18: 19) sts. Pull up tight and fasten off securely. Join back seam, reversing seam for first 1¹/₂in, 4cm, for turn-back. Fold 1¹/₄in, 3cm, to RS around lower edge. Using yarn A, make a pompon 1¹/₂in, 4cm, diameter and attach to top of Hat.

# Scarf

With 3³/₄mm (US size 5/UK No.9) needles and yarn A, cast on 27 (31: 53) sts.

Work in rib as given for Hat for 10¹/₄ (11³/₄: 13¹/₄)in, 26 (30: 34)cm, ending with a WS row.

Break off yarn A and join in yarn B.

Cont in rib until Scarf measures 20¹/₂ (23¹/₂: 26³/₄)in, 52 (60: 68)cm, ending with a WS row.

Break off yarn B and join in yarn C.

Cont in rib until Scarf measures 30³/₄ (35¹/₂: 40)in, 78 (90: 102)cm, ending with a WS row.

Bind (cast) off in rib.

Run gathering threads across both ends of Scarf, pull up tight and fasten off securely. Using yarn C, make two pompons 1¹/₂in, 4cm, in diameter and attach to ends of Scarf.

# hooded striped sweater

Create a rainbow for your little ray of sunshine. Knit this sweater in vibrant colors to brighten up a rainy day. For a more laid-back look, go for pastel shades.

## Sizes and finished knitted measurements

|  | Bear | | Child | | |
|---|---|---|---|---|---|
| To fit size/age | medium | 4–5 | 6–7 | 8–9 | yrs |
| Chest size | 13 | 24 | 26 | 28 | in |
|  | 33 | 61 | 66 | 71 | cm |
| Actual width | $7^3/4$ | $14^1/8$ | $15^1/8$ | $16^1/4$ | in |
|  | $19^1/2$ | 36 | $38^1/2$ | $41^1/2$ | cm |
| Length to shoulder | $6^1/4$ | $14^1/2$ | 16 | $17^3/4$ | in |
|  | 16 | 37 | 41 | 45 | cm |
| Sleeve length | 5 | $10^1/2$ | $12^1/4$ | $13^3/4$ | in |
|  | 13 | 27 | 31 | 35 | cm |

## Materials

**YARN:** 1 (2: 3: 4) x 25g (1oz) balls of Rowan Kidsilk Haze (used DOUBLE throughout) in A (dark fuchsia), 1 (1: 2: 2) balls in each of B (dark purple) and E (lime green), and 1 (2: 3: 3) balls in each of C (dark lilac) and D (light turquoise)

**KNITTING NEEDLES:** Pair each of 3mm (US size 2–3/UK No.11) and $3^3/4$mm (US size 5/UK No.9) needles

## Abbreviations

See page 93.

## Stitch gauge/tension

23 sts and 32 rows to 4in, 10cm, measured over stockinette (stocking) stitch on $3^3/_-$mm (US size 5/UK No.9) needles using yarn DOUBLE.

## Note

All yarns are used DOUBLE throughout.

## Back

With 3mm (US size 2–3/UK No.11) needles and yarn A, cast on 45 (83: 89: 95) sts.
**ROW 1 (RS):** K1, *p1, k1; rep from * to end.
**ROW 2:** P1, *k1, p1; rep from * to end.
These 2 rows form rib.
Work in rib for a further 4 (6: 6: 6) rows, ending with a WS row.
Change to $3^3/4$mm (US size 5/UK No.9) needles.
Starting with a k row, now work in striped stockinette (stocking) stitch as follows:
Using yarn B, work 2 (4: 4: 4) rows.
Using yarn C, work 4 (8: 8: 8) rows.
Using yarn D, work 2 (4: 4: 4) rows.
Using yarn E, work 2 (4: 4: 4) rows.
Using yarn A, work 2 (4: 4: 4) rows.
Using yarn C, work 2 (4: 4: 4) rows.
Using yarn D, work 4 (8: 8: 8) rows.
Using yarn A, work 2 (4: 4: 4) rows.
These 20 (40: 40: 40) rows form striped stockinette (stocking) stitch.
Cont in striped stockinette (stocking) stitch until Back measures $3^1/4$ (9: $10^1/4$: $11^1/2$)in, 8.5 (23: 26: 29)cm, ending with a WS row.

### Shape armholes

Keeping stripes correct, bind (cast) off 3 sts at beg of next 2 rows. 39 (77: 83: 89) sts.
Dec 0 (1: 1: 1) st at each end of next 5 rows. 39 (67: 73: 79) sts.
Cont straight until armhole measures 3 ($5^1/2$: 6: $6^1/4$)in, 7.5 (14: 15: 16)cm, ending with a WS row.

### Shape shoulders

Bind (cast) off 5 (9: 10: 11) sts at beg of next 4 rows.
Bind (cast) off rem 19 (31: 33: 35) sts.

## Front

Work as given for Back until 8 (16: 16: 18) rows fewer have been worked than on Back to start of shoulder shaping, ending with a WS row.

### Shape neck

**NEXT ROW (RS):** K15 (26: 29: 31) and turn, leaving rem sts on a holder. Work on this set of sts only for first side of neck.

Dec 1 st at neck edge of next 5 (6: 7: 7) rows, then on foll 0 (2: 2: 2) alt rows. 10 (18: 20: 22) sts.

Work 2 (5: 4: 6) rows, ending with a WS row.

### Shape shoulder

Bind (cast) off 5 (9: 10: 11) sts at beg of next row.

Work 1 row.

Bind (cast) off rem 5 (9: 10: 11) sts.

With RS facing, rejoin appropriate yarn to rem sts, bind (cast) off center 9 (15: 15: 17) sts, k to end.

Complete to match first side, reversing shaping, working an extra row before start of shoulder shaping.

## Sleeves (make 2)

With 3mm (US size 2–3/UK No.11) needles and yarn A, cast on 31 (45: 47: 49) sts.

Work in rib as given for Back for 6 (8: 8: 8) rows, ending with a WS row.

Change to 3³/₄mm (US size 5/UK No.9) needles.

Starting with a k row, now work in striped stockinette (stocking) stitch as given for Back, shaping sides by inc 1 st at each end of 9th (7th : 7th: 7th) and every foll 10th (7th: 8th: 9th) row until there are 37 (65: 67: 69) sts.

Cont straight until Sleeve measures 5 (10¹/₂: 12¹/₄: 13³/₄)in, 13 (27: 31: 35)cm, ending with a WS row.

### Shape top

Keeping stripes correct, bind (cast) off 0 (3: 3: 3) sts at beg of next 2 rows. 37 (59: 61: 63) sts.

Dec 1 st at each end of next and foll 3 alt rows, then on foll row, ending with a WS row.

Bind (cast) off rem 27 (49: 51: 53) sts.

## Hood

With 3mm (US size 2–3/UK No.11) needles and yarn A, cast on 81 (119: 123: 127) sts.

Work in rib as given for Back for 6 (8: 8: 8) rows, inc 1 st at end of last row and ending with a WS row. 82 (120: 124: 128) sts.

Change to 3³/₄mm (US size 5/UK No.9) needles.

Starting with a k row, now work in striped stockinette (stocking) stitch as given for Back, shaping neck edge by dec 1 st at each end of 2nd (3rd: 3rd: 3rd) and every foll 3rd row until 68 (102: 106: 110) sts rem.

Cont straight until Hood measures 4 (6¹/₂: 7: 7¹/₂)in, 10 (17: 18: 19)cm, ending with a WS row.

### Shape back

Place marker between center sts of last row.

**NEXT ROW (RS):** K to within 2 sts of marker, k2tog, slip marker to right needle, k2tog tbl, k to end.

**NEXT ROW:** Purl.

Rep last 2 rows twice more. 62 (96: 100: 104) sts.

**NEXT ROW (RS):** K to within 2 sts of marker, k2tog, slip marker to right needle, k2tog tbl, k to end.

**NEXT ROW:** P to within 2 sts of marker, p2tog tbl, slip marker to right needle, p2tog, p to end.

Rep last 2 rows 1 (3: 3: 3) times more.

Bind (cast) off rem 54 (80: 84: 88) sts.

## Making up

Join shoulder seams. Join back seam of Hood. Matching hood seam to center back neck and with cast-on edges of Hood meeting at center front neck, sew shaped row end edges of Hood to neck edge, easing in fullness. Matching center of bind-off (cast-off) edge of Sleeves to shoulder seams, sew Sleeves to Back and Front. Join side and sleeve seams.

Bear's sweater: Make a twisted cord 10¹/₄in, 26cm, long using yarn A and two pompons, each 1¹/₄in, 3cm, in diameter using all colors. Attach pompons to ends of cord and then attach center of cord to front neck.

# *heart jacket*

This will delight child and knitter alike with its pastel pink shades and pretty hearts. Knitted in lovely soft tones to capture the hearts of your little ones. The pattern will also look good in brighter colors.

## Sizes and finished knitted measurements

|  | Child |  |
|---|---|---|
| To fit age | 4–5 | yrs |
| Chest size | 26 | in |
|  | 56 | cm |
| Actual width | 15 | in |
|  | 38 | cm |
| Length | 15¼ | in |
|  | 39 | cm |
| Sleeve length | 10½ | in |
|  | 27 | cm |

## Materials

**YARN:** 6 × 50g (1¾oz) balls of Rowan Wool Cotton in A (cream), 1 ball in each of B (grey), C (camel), D (lavender) and E (pink), and scraps of F (brown) for embroidery

**KNITTING NEEDLES:** Pair each of 3mm (US size 2–3/UK No.11) and 3¾mm (US size 5/UK No.9) needles

**BUTTONS:** 5

## Abbreviations

See page 93.

## Stitch gauge/tension

24 sts and 32 rows to 4in, 10cm, measured over stockinette (stocking) stitch on 3¾mm (US size 5/UK No.9) needles.

## Note

When working from chart, work odd numbered rows as knit rows, reading chart from right to left, and even numbered rows as purl rows, reading chart from left to right.

## Back

With 3mm (US size 2–3/UK No.11) needles and yarn B, cast on 91 sts.

**\*\*ROW 1 (WS):** Knit.

Join in yarn A.

**ROWS 2 AND 3:** Using yarn A knit.

**ROWS 4 AND 5:** Using yarn B knit.

**ROWS 6 TO 9:** As rows 2 to 5.

Change to 3¾mm (US size 5/UK No.9) needles.\*\*

Starting and ending rows as indicated, work 42 rows in patt from chart, ending with a WS row.

Break off all contrasts and cont using yarn A only.

Cont in stockinette (stocking) stitch until Back measures 9½ in, 24cm, ending with a WS row.

### Shape armholes

Bind (cast) off 3 sts at beg of next 2 rows. 85 sts.

Dec 1 st at each end of next 4 rows. 77 sts.

Cont straight until armhole measures 6in, 15cm, ending with a WS row.

### Shape shoulders

Bind (cast) off 12 sts at beg of next 4 rows.

Bind (cast) off rem 29 sts.

## Left Front

With 3mm (US size 2–3/UK No.11) needles and yarn B, cast on 51 sts.

## bottom of jacket

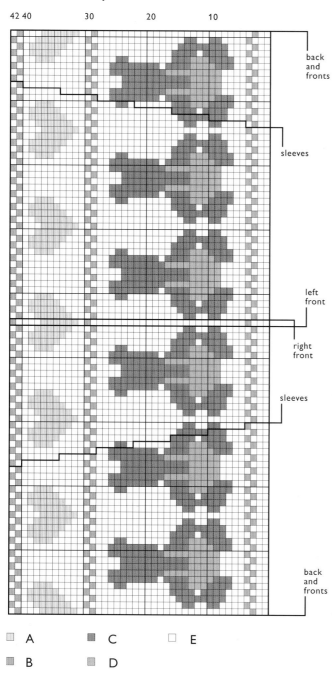

| A | C | E |
|---|---|---|
| B | D | |

**ROW 1 (WS):** Knit.

Join in yarn A.

**ROWS 2 AND 3:** Using yarn A knit.

**ROW 4:** Using yarn B k to last 4 sts, yfwd, k2tog, k2.

**ROW 5:** Using yarn B knit.

**ROWS 6 AND 7:** Using yarn A knit.

**ROW 8:** Using yarn B knit.

**ROW 9:** Using yarn B k6 and slip these 6 sts onto a holder; inc in next st, k to end. 46 sts.

Change to $3^3/_4$ mm (US size 5/UK No.9) needles.

Starting and ending rows as indicated, work 42 rows in patt from chart, ending with a WS row.

Break off all contrasts and cont using yarn A only.

Cont in stockinette (stocking) stitch until Left Front matches Back to start of armhole shaping, ending with a WS row.

**Shape armhole**

Bind (cast) off 3 sts at beg of next row. 43 sts.

Work 1 row.

Dec 1 st at armhole edge of next 4 rows. 39 sts.

**Shape front slope**

Dec 1 st at end of next and foll 11 alt rows, then on every foll 4th row until 24 sts rem.

Cont straight until Left Front matches Back to start of shoulder shaping, ending with a WS row.

**Shape shoulder**

Bind (cast) off 12 sts at beg of next row.

Work 1 row.

Bind (cast) off rem 12 sts.

# Right Front

With 3mm (US size 2–3/UK No.11) needles and yarn B, cast on 51 sts.

**ROW 1 (WS):** Knit.

Join in yarn A.

**ROWS 2 AND 3:** Using yarn A knit.

**ROWS 4 AND 5:** Using yarn B knit.

**ROWS 6 AND 7:** Using yarn A knit.

**ROW 8:** Using yarn B knit.

**ROW 9:** Using yarn B k to last 7 sts, inc in next st and turn, leaving last 6 sts on a holder. 46 sts.

Complete to match Left Front, reversing shapings, working an extra row before start of armhole and shoulder shaping.

## Sleeves (make 2)

With 3mm (US size 2–3/UK No.11) needles and yarn B, cast on 46 sts.
Work as given for Back from ** to **.
Starting and ending rows as indicated, work 42 rows in patt from chart and at same time inc 1 st at each end of 5th and every foll 6th row, ending with a WS row. 60 sts.
Break off all contrasts and cont using yarn A only.
Cont in stockinette (stocking) stitch, shaping sides by inc 1 st at each end of 5th and every foll 6th row until there are 68 sts.
Cont straight until Sleeve measures 10½in, 27cm, ending with a WS row.

### Shape top

Bind (cast) off 3 sts at beg of next 2 rows. 62 sts.
Dec 1 st at each end of next and foll 2 alt rows.
Work 1 row, ending with a WS row.
Bind (cast) off rem 56 sts.

## Right Front Band and Collar

Join shoulder seams.
Slip 6 sts left on right front holder onto 3mm (US size 2–3/UK No.11) needles and rejoin yarn B with WS facing.
Knit 1 row.
Break off yarn B and join in yarn A.
**Cont in garter stitch until Band, when slightly stretched, fits up front opening edge to start of front slope shaping, sewing in place as you go along.

### Shape collar

Inc 1 st at inner (attached) edge of next and every foll alt row until there are 26 sts.
Cont straight until Collar, unstretched, fits up right front slope to shoulder, sewing in place as you go along and ending at outer (unattached) edge.
**NEXT ROW:** K to last 3 sts, bring yarn to front of work between needles, slip next st onto right needle and take yarn to back of work between needles, slip st now on right needle back onto left needle and turn.
Knit 3 rows.
Rep last 4 rows until Collar fits across to center back neck.
Bind (cast) off knitwise.
Mark positions for 5 buttons on this band—first to come level with buttonhole already worked in Left Front, last to come ³⁄₈in, 1cm, below start of front slope shaping and rem 3 buttons evenly spaced between.

## Left Front Band and Collar

Slip 6 sts left on left front holder onto 3mm (US size 2–3/UK No.11) needles and rejoin yarn A with RS facing.
Work to match Right Front Band and Collar from **, with the addition of a further 4 buttonholes worked as follows:
**BUTTONHOLE ROW (RS):** K3, yfwd, k2tog, k1.

## Making up

Join center back seam of collar sections, then sew edge of Collar to back neck edge. Matching center of bound-off (cast-off) edge of Sleeves to shoulder seams, sew Sleeves to Back and Fronts. Join side and sleeve seams. Sew on buttons.

### Embroidery

Using yarn F and following photograph as a guide, embroider french knot eyes, satin stitch noses and straight stitch mouths onto bears.

# *bear's heart waistcoat*

### Sizes and finished knitted measurements

|  | Bear |  |
|---|---|---|
| To fit size | medium |  |
| Chest size | 13 | in |
|  | 33 | cm |
| Actual width | 7³⁄₈ | in |
|  | 19½ | cm |
| Length | 5½ | in |
|  | 14 | cm |

### Materials

**YARN:** 2 × 50g (1¾oz) balls of Rowan Wool Cotton in A (cream), 1 ball in B (grey), and scrap of C (pink) for heart motifs
**KNITTING NEEDLES:** Pair each of 3mm (US size 2–3/UK No.11) and 3¾mm (US size 5/UK No.9) needles
**BUTTONS:** 4

### Abbreviations

See page 93.

### Stitch gauge/tension

24 sts and 32 rows to 4in, 10cm, measured over stockinette (stocking) stitch on 3¾mm (US size 5/UK No.9) needles.

## Note

When working from chart, work odd numbered rows as knit rows, reading chart from right to left, and even numbered rows as purl rows, reading chart from left to right.

## Back

With 3mm (US size 2–3/UK No.11) needles and yarn B, cast on 47 sts.
**ROW 1 (WS):** Knit.
Join in yarn A.
**ROWS 2 AND 3:** Using yarn A knit.
**ROWS 4 AND 5:** Using yarn B knit.
Break off yarn B and cont using yarn A only.
**ROWS 6 AND 7:** Knit.
Change to $3^3/_4$mm (US size 5/UK No.9) needles.**
Starting with a k row, work in stockinette (stocking) stitch until Back measures $2^3/_4$in, 7cm, ending with a WS row.
**Shape armholes**
Bind (cast) off 5 sts at beg of next 2 rows. 37 sts.
Dec 1 st at each end of next 4 rows. 29 sts.
Cont straight until armhole measures $2^3/_4$in, 7cm, ending with a WS row.
**Shape shoulders**
Bind (cast) off 7 sts at beg of next 2 rows.
Bind (cast) off rem 15 sts.

## Left Front

With 3mm (US size 2–3/UK No.11) needles and yarn B, cast on 28 sts.
**ROW 1 (WS):** Knit.
Join in yarn A.

**ROWS 2 AND 3:** Using yarn A knit.
**ROW 4:** Using yarn B k to last 3 sts, yfwd, k2tog, k1.
**ROW 5:** Using yarn B knit.
Break off yarn B and cont using yarn A only.
**ROW 6:** Knit.
**ROW 7:** K5 and slip these 5 sts onto a holder, inc in next st, k to end. 24 sts.
Change to $3^3/_4$mm (US size 5/UK No.9) needles.
Starting with a k row, work in stockinette (stocking) stitch until Left Front matches Back to start of armhole shaping, ending with a WS row.
**Shape armhole**
Bind (cast) off 5 sts at beg of next row. 19 sts.
Work 1 row.
Dec 1 st at armhole edge of next 4 rows. 15 sts.
**Shape front slope**
Dec 1 st at end of next row and at same edge of every foll row until 7 sts rem.
Cont straight until Left Front matches Back to start of shoulder shaping, ending with a WS row.
**Shape shoulders**
Bind (cast) off rem 7 sts.

## Right Front

With 3mm (US size 2–3/UK No.11) needles and yarn B, cast on 28 sts.
**ROW 1 (WS):** Knit.
Join in yarn A.
**ROWS 2 AND 3:** Using yarn A knit.
**ROWS 4 AND 5:** Using yarn B knit.
Break off yarn B and cont using yarn A only.
**ROW 6:** Knit.
**ROW 7:** K to last 6 sts, inc in next st and turn, leaving rem 5 sts on a holder. 24 sts.
Complete to match Left Front, reversing shapings, working an extra row before start of armhole and shoulder shaping.

## Pockets (make 2)

With 3mm (US size 2–3/UK No.11) needles and yarn A, cast on 13 sts.
Starting with a k row, work in stockinette (stocking) stitch for 2 rows, ending with a WS row.
**ROW 3:** K2, work next 9 sts as row 1 of Heart Chart, k2.
**ROW 4:** P2, work next 9 sts as row 2 of Heart Chart, p2.
Cont as set until all 8 rows of Heart Chart have been completed,

## teddy's pocket

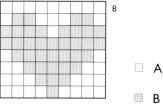

□ A

▨ B

ending with a WS row.
Starting with a k row, work in stockinette (stocking) stitch for 2 rows, ending with a WS row.
Join in yarn B.
**ROWS 13 AND 14:** Using yarn B knit.
**ROWS 15 AND 16:** Using yarn A knit.
**ROW 17:** Using yarn B knit.
Using yarn B, bind (cast) off knitwise.

## Right Front Band

Join shoulder seams.
Slip 5 sts left on Right Front holder onto 3mm (US size 2–3/UK No.11) needles and rejoin yarn A with WS facing.
**Cont in garter stitch until Band, when slightly stretched, fits up front opening edge, up front slope and across to center back neck, sewing in place as you go along.
Bind (cast) off.
Mark positions for 4 buttons on this band—first to come level with buttonhole already worked in Left Front, last to come ³/₈in, 1cm, below start of front slope shaping and rem 2 buttons evenly spaced between.

## Left Front Band

Slip 5 sts left on Left Front holder onto 3mm (US size 2–3/UK No.11) needles and rejoin yarn A with RS facing.
Work to match Right Front Band from **, with the addition of a further 3 buttonholes worked as follows:
**BUTTONHOLE ROW (RS):** K2, yfwd, k2tog, k1.

## Armhole Borders (both alike)

With RS facing and 3mm (US size 2–3/UK No.11) needles, pick up and knit 42 sts evenly around armhole edge.
**ROW 1 (WS):** Knit.

Join in yarn B.
**ROWS 2 AND 3:** Using yarn B knit.
**ROWS 4 AND 5:** Using yarn A knit.
**ROW 6:** Using yarn B knit.
Using yarn B, bind (cast) off knitwise.

## Making up

Join ends of bands at center back neck. Join side seams to Armhole Borders. Sew on buttons.

# Aran sweater and vest

This single colored, multi-textured sweater and vest will go with anything.

## Sizes and finished knitted measurements

| | Bear | | | Child | | | |
|---|---|---|---|---|---|---|---|
| To fit size/age | small | medium | large | 1–2 | 3–4 | 4–5 | yrs |
| Chest size | 13 | 16 | 18 | 22 | 24 | 27 | in |
| | 33 | 41 | 46 | 56 | 61 | 69 | cm |
| Actual width | $8^1/_4$ | $9^1/_2$ | $11^1/_4$ | $13^1/_4$ | $14^1/_8$ | $16^1/_8$ | in |
| | 21 | 24 | $28^1/_2$ | $33^1/_2$ | 36 | 41 | cm |
| Length to shoulder | $4^3/_4$ | 7 | $9^3/_4$ | $10^1/_4$ | $12^1/_2$ | $14^1/_2$ | in |
| | 12 | 18 | 25 | 26 | 32 | 37 | cm |
| Sleeve length | – | – | – | $7^3/_4$ | $8^1/_2$ | $9^1/_2$ | in |
| | – | – | – | 20 | 22 | 24 | cm |

## Materials

**YARN:** 6 (7: 8) x 50g ($1^3/_4$oz) balls of Jaeger Matchmaker Merino Aran in cream

**KNITTING NEEDLES:** Pair each of 4mm (US size 6/UK No.8) and $4^1/_2$mm (US size 7/UK No.7) needles
Cable needle

## Abbreviations

See page 93.

C3B = slip next st onto cable needle and leave at back of work, k2, then k1 from cable needle

C3F = slip next 2 sts onto cable needle and leave at front of work, k1, then k2 from cable needle

C4B = slip next 2 sts onto cable needle and leave at back of work, k2, then k2 from cable needle

C4F = slip next 2 sts onto cable needle and leave at front of work, k2, then k2 from cable needle

Cr3R = slip next st onto cable needle and leave at back of work, k2, then p1 from cable needle

Cr3L = slip next 2 sts onto cable needle and leave at front of work, p1, then k2 from cable needle.

MB = (k1, p1, k1, p1, k1) all into next st, turn, p5, turn, lift 2nd, 3rd, 4th and 5th sts on left needle over first st and off needle, then k rem st on left needle.

## Stitch gauge/tension

26 sts and 26 rows to 4in, 10cm, measured over pattern, 19 sts and 25 rows to 4in, 10cm, measured over stockinette (stocking) stitch on $4^1/_2$mm (US size 7/UK No.7) needles.

## Cable Panel A (16 sts)

**ROW 1 (RS):** P4, k8, p4.

**ROW 2:** K4, p8, k4.

**ROW 3:** P4, k1, C3B, C3F, k1, p4.

**ROW 4:** K4, p3, k1, p4, k4.

**ROW 5:** P4, C3B, p1, k1, Cr3L, p4.

**ROW 6:** K4, p3, k1, p1, k1, p2, k4.

**ROW 7:** P3, Cr3R, (k1, p1) twice, C3F, p3.

**ROW 8:** K3, p2, (k1, p1) twice, k1, p3, k3.

**ROW 9:** P2, C3B, (p1, k1) 3 times, Cr3L, p2.

**ROW 10:** K2, p3, (k1, p1) 3 times, k1, p2, k2.

**ROW 11:** P2, Cr3L, (p1, k1) 3 times, Cr3R, p2.

**ROW 12:** As row 8.

**ROW 13:** P3, Cr3L, (k1, p1) twice, Cr3R, p3.

**ROW 14:** As row 6.

**ROW 15:** P4, Cr3L, p1, k1, Cr3R, p4.

**ROW 16:** K5, p2, k1, p3, k5.

**ROW 17:** P5, Cr3L, Cr3R, p5.

**ROW 18:** K6, p4, k6.

**ROW 19:** P4, C4B, C4F, p4.

**ROW 20:** As row 2.

**ROW 21:** As row 1.

**ROW 22:** As row 2.

**ROW 23:** As row 19.

**ROW 24:** As row 2.

These 24 rows form Cable Panel A.

## Cable Panel B (9 sts)

**ROW 1 (RS):** K9.

**ROW 2:** P9.

**ROW 3:** C4B, k1, C4B.

**ROW 4:** P9.

**ROW 5:** K4, MB, k4.

**ROW 6:** P9.

**ROW 7:** K3, MB, k1, MB, k3.

**ROW 8:** P9.

These 8 rows form Cable Panel B.

## Back

With 4mm (US size 6/UK No.8) needles, cast on 75 (81: 93) sts.

**RIB ROW 1 (RS):** K1, *p1, k1; rep from * to end.

**RIB ROW 2:** P1, *k1, p1; rep from * to end.

These 2 rows form rib.

Work in rib for a further 11 rows, ending with a RS row.

**ROW 14 (WS):** Rib 7 (8: 8), inc in next st, *rib 14 (15: 18), inc in next st; rep from * to last 7 (8: 8) sts, rib to end. 80 (86: 98) sts.

Change to 4mm (US size 6/UK No.8) needles.

**NEXT ROW (RS):** (K1, p1) 6 (8: 11) times, k1 (0: 0), p2, k2, p2, work next 9 sts as row 1 of Cable Panel B, p2, k2, work next 16 sts as row 1 of Cable Panel A, k2, p2, work next 9 sts as row 1 of Cable Panel B, p2, k2, p2, k1 (0: 0), (p1, k1) 6 (8: 11) times.

**NEXT ROW:** (K1, p1) 6 (8: 11) times, k3 (2: 2), p2, k2, work next 9 sts as row 2 of Cable Panel B, k2, p2, work next 16 sts as row 2 of Cable Panel A, p2, k2, work next 9 sts as row 2 of Cable Panel B, k2, p2, k3 (2: 2), (p1, k1) 6 (8: 11) times.

These 2 rows form patt.

Cont in patt until Back measures 5$^1$/$_2$ (7$^1$/$_2$: 9$^1$/$_2$)in, 14 (19: 24)cm, ending with a WS row.

### Shape armholes

Keeping patt correct, bind (cast) off 4 (5: 5) sts at beg of next 2 rows. 72 (76: 88) sts.

Dec 1 st at each end of next 4 rows. 64 (68: 80) sts.

Cont straight until armhole measures 4³/₄ (5: 5)in, 12 (13: 13)cm, ending with a WS row.

### Shape shoulders

Bind (cast) off 17 (17: 21) sts at beg of next 2 rows.

Leave rem 30 (34: 38) sts on a holder.

## Front

Work as given for Back until armhole measures 2¹/₄ (2³/₄: 2³/₄)in, 6 (7: 7)cm, ending with a WS row.

### Shape neck

**NEXT ROW (RS):** Patt 24 (25: 31) sts and turn, leaving rem sts on a holder.

Work on this set of sts only for first side of neck.

Dec 1 st at neck edge of next 7 (8: 10) rows. 17 (17: 21) sts.

Cont straight until Front matches Back to start of shoulder shaping, ending with a WS row.

### Shape shoulder

Bind (cast) off rem 17 (17: 21) sts.

With RS facing, slip center 16 (18: 18) sts onto a holder, rejoin yarn to rem sts, patt to end.

Complete to match first side, reversing shaping, working an extra row before start of shoulder shaping.

## Sleeves (make 2)

With 4mm (US size 6/UK No.8) needles, cast on 41 (43: 45) sts.

Work in rib as given for Back for 13 rows, ending with a RS row.

**ROW 14 (WS):** Rib 4 (3: 4), inc in next st, *rib 7 (8: 8), inc in next st; rep from * to last 4 (3: 4) sts, rib to end. 46 (48: 50) sts.

Change to 4mm (US size 6/UK No.8) needles.

**NEXT ROW (RS):** K0 (1: 2), p2, work next 9 sts as row 1 of Cable Panel B, p2, k2, work next 16 sts as row 1 of Cable Panel A, k2, p2, work next 9 sts as row 1 of Cable Panel B, p2, k0 (1: 2).

**NEXT ROW:** P0 (1: 2), k2, work next 9 sts as row 2 of Cable Panel B, k2, p2, work next 16 sts as row 2 of Cable Panel A, p2, k2, work next 9 sts as row 2 of Cable Panel B, k2, p0 (1: 2).

These 2 rows set position of patt as given for Back.

Cont in patt, shaping sides by inc 1 st at each end of next and every foll 3ʳᵈ (3ʳᵈ: 4ᵗʰ) row until there are 64 (70: 70) sts, taking inc sts into patt.

Cont straight until Sleeve measures 7³/₄ (8¹/₂: 9¹/₂)in, 20 (22: 24)cm, ending with a WS row.

Bind (cast) off in patt.

## Neckband

Join right shoulder seam.

With RS facing and 4mm (US size 6/UK No.8) needles, pick up and knit 12 sts down left side of neck, knit across 16 (18: 18) sts left on front holder, pick up and knit 12 sts up right side of neck, then knit across 30 (34: 38) sts left on back holder. 70 (76: 80) sts.

Starting with a p row, work in stockinette (stocking) stitch for 11 rows, ending with a WS row.

Bind (cast) off.

## Making up

Join left shoulder seam to Neckband, reversing seam for roll. Matching center of bind-off (cast-off) edge of Sleeves to shoulder seams, sew Sleeves to Back and Front. Join side and sleeve seams.

# *bear's vest*

### Materials

**YARN:** 1 (2: 3: 3: 3: 4) × 50g (1³/₄oz) balls of Jaeger Matchmaker Merino Aran in cream

**KNITTING NEEDLES:** Pair each of 4mm (US size 6/UK No.8) and 4¹/₂mm (US size 7/UK No.7) needles

Cable needle

### Abbreviations

See Sweater on page 65 and page 93.

### Stitch gauge/tension

19 sts and 25 rows to 4in, 10cm, measured over stockinette (stocking) stitch on 4¹/₂mm (US size 7/UK No.7) needles.

## Cable Panel A (16 sts)

Work as given for Cable Panel A of Sweater.

## Back

With 4mm (US size 6/UK No.8) needles, cast on 37 (43: 51: 61: 65: 75) sts.

**RIB ROW 1 (RS):** K1, *p1, k1; rep from * to end.

**RIB ROW 2:** P1, *k1, p1; rep from * to end.

These 2 rows form rib.

Work in rib for a further 6 (8: 8: 10: 10: 10) rows, inc 3 sts evenly across last row and ending with a WS row. 40 (46: 54: 64: 68: 78) sts.

Change to 4¹/₂mm (US size 7/UK No.7) needles.**

Starting with a k row, work in stockinette (stocking) stitch until Back measures 2 (4: 5½: 5½: 7½: 9½)in, 5 (10: 14: 14: 19: 24)cm, ending with a WS row.

### Shape armholes

Bind (cast) off 3 (3: 4: 4: 5: 5) sts at beg of next 2 rows. 34 (40: 46: 56: 58: 68) sts.

Dec 1 st at each end of next 2 (3: 4: 4: 4: 4) rows. 30 (34: 38: 48: 50: 60) sts.

Cont straight until armhole measures 2¾ (3: 4¼: 4¾: 5: 5)in, 7 (8: 11: 12: 13: 13)cm, ending with a WS row.

### Shape shoulders

Bind (cast) off 6 (8: 8: 12: 12: 16) sts at beg of next 2 rows.

Leave rem 18 (18: 22: 24: 26: 28) sts on a holder.

## Front

Work as given for Back to **.

**NEXT ROW (RS):** K12 (15: 19: 24: 26: 31), work next 16 sts as row 1 of Cable Panel A, k to end.

**NEXT ROW:** P12 (15: 19: 24: 26: 31), work next 16 sts as row 2 of Cable Panel A, p to end.

These 2 rows set position of Cable Panel A with stockinette (stocking) stitch at sides.

Cont as set until Front matches Back to start of armhole shaping, ending with a WS row.

### Shape armholes

Keeping patt correct, bind (cast) off 3 (3: 4: 4: 5: 5) sts at beg of next 2 rows. 34 (40: 46: 56: 58: 68) sts.

Dec 1 st at each end of next 2 (3: 4: 4: 4: 4) rows. 30 (34: 38: 48: 50: 60) sts.

Cont straight until armhole measures 1½ (2: 2¾: 2¾: 3: 3)in, 4 (5: 7: 7: 8: 8)cm, ending with a WS row.

### Shape neck

**NEXT ROW (RS):** Patt 11 (12: 12: 16: 16: 19) sts and turn, leaving rem sts on a holder.

Work on this set of sts only for first side of neck.

Dec 1 st at neck edge of next 5 (4: 4: 4: 4: 3) rows. 6 (8: 8: 12: 12: 16) sts.

Cont straight until Front matches Back to start of shoulder shaping, ending with a WS row.

### Shape shoulder

Bind (cast) off rem 6 (8: 8: 12: 12: 16) sts.

With RS facing, slip center 8 (10: 14: 16: 18: 22) sts onto a holder, rejoin yarn to rem sts, patt to end.

Complete to match first side, reversing shaping, working an extra row before start of shoulder shaping.

## Neckband

Join right shoulder seam.

With RS facing and 4mm (US size 6/UK No.8) needles, pick up and knit 7 (7: 10: 12: 12: 12) sts down left side of neck, knit across 8 (10: 14: 16: 18: 22) sts left on front holder, pick up and knit 7 (7: 10: 12: 12: 12) sts up right side of neck, then knit across 18 (18: 22: 24: 26: 28) sts left on back holder. 40 (42: 56: 64: 68: 74) sts.

Starting with p row, work in stockinette (stocking) stitch for 7 (7: 7: 9: 9: 9) rows, ending with a WS row.

Bind (cast) off knitwise.

## Armhole Borders (both alike)

Join left shoulder to Neckband, reversing seam for Neckband roll.

With RS facing and 4mm (US size 6/UK No.8) needles, pick up and knit 39 (45: 59: 65: 71: 71) sts evenly all round armhole edge.

Bind (cast) off knitwise.

## Making up

Join side seams to Armhole Borders.

# ballerina wrapover top

Knit this luxurious ballet top for your little dancing queen and her troupe of teddies.
A sparkly crochet edging defines the wrapover shape and trims the sleeves.

## Sizes and finished knitted measurements

| | | Bear | | | Child | | | |
|---|---|---|---|---|---|---|---|---|
| To fit size/age | small | medium | large | 1–2 | 2–3 | 4–5 | 6–7 | yrs |
| Chest size | 10 | 12 | 16 | 20 | 22 | 24 | 26 | in |
| | 26 | 31 | 41 | 51 | 56 | 61 | 66 | cm |
| Actual measurement | 5$^3$/$_4$ | 6$^3$/$_4$ | 8$^3$/$_5$ | 11$^3$/$_4$ | 12$^3$/$_4$ | 13$^3$/$_4$ | 15 | in |
| | 14$^1$/$_2$ | 17 | 22 | 30 | 32$^1$/$_2$ | 35 | 38 | cm |
| Length to shoulder | 3$^1$/$_2$ | 4$^3$/$_4$ | 6 | 9 | 10$^1$/$_2$ | 11$^1$/$_2$ | 13 | in |
| | 9 | 12 | 15 | 23 | 27 | 29 | 33 | cm |
| Sleeve length | 3 | 4$^1$/$_4$ | 5 | 7$^1$/$_2$ | 9 | 10$^1$/$_2$ | 12$^1$/$_4$ | in |
| | 8 | 11 | 13 | 19 | 23 | 27 | 31 | cm |

## Materials

**YARN:** 1 (2: 3: 3: 4: 5: 5) x 25g (1oz) balls of Rowan Kidsilk Haze
(used DOUBLE throughout) in dark lilac, camel or denim blue
1 x 25g (1oz) ball of Rowan Lurex Shimmer in matching color for
crochet edging

**KNITTING NEEDLES:** Pair each of 3mm (US size 2–3/UK No.11) and
3$^3$/$_4$mm (US size 5/UK No.9) needles

**CROCHET HOOK:** 3mm (US size D3/UK No.11) crochet hook

## Abbreviations

See page 93.

## Stitch gauge/tension

23 sts and 32 rows to 4in, 10cm, measured over stockinette (stocking)
stitch on 3$^3$/$_4$mm (US size 5/UK No.9) needles using yarn DOUBLE.

## Note

Rowan Kidsilk Haze is used DOUBLE throughout.

## Left Front

With 3$^3$/$_4$mm (US size 5/UK No.9) needles, cast on 29 (35: 47: 63:
69: 75: 81) sts.
Starting with a k row, work in stockinette (stocking) stitch for
6 rows, ending with a WS row.

### Shape front slope

Place marker at beg of last row.
Dec 1 st at marked front opening edge of next 19 (17: 23: 19: 15:
17: 11) rows, then on foll 1 (7: 9: 5: 11: 12: 20) alt rows. 9 (11: 15: 39:
43: 46: 50) sts.
Work 1 row, ending with a WS row.

### Child's top only
### Shape armhole

Bind (cast) off 6 sts at beg and dec 1 st at end of next row. (32: 36:
39: 43) sts.
Dec 1 st at front slope edge of 2$^{nd}$ and foll (14: 16: 17: 19) alt rows.
(17: 19: 21: 23) sts.
Cont straight until armhole measures (4$^3$/$_4$: 5: 5$^1$/$_2$: 6)in, (12: 13: 14:

15)cm, ending with a WS row.

**All tops**

**Shape shoulder**

Bind (cast) off 4 (5: 7: 6: 6: 7: 8) sts at beg of next and foll 0 (0: 0: 1: 1: 1: 1) alt row.

Work 1 row.

Bind (cast) off rem 5 (6: 8: 5: 7: 7: 7) sts.

## Right Front

Work as given for Left Front, reversing shapings, working an extra row before start of armhole (for child only) and shoulder shaping.

## Back

With 3³/₄mm (US size 5/UK No.9) needles, cast on 33 (39: 51: 69: 75: 81: 87) sts.

Starting with a k row, work in stockinette (stocking) stitch as follows:

**Child's top only**

Cont straight until Back matches Fronts to start of armhole shaping, ending with a WS row.

**Shape armholes**

Bind (cast) off 6 sts at beg of next 2 rows. (57: 63: 69: 75) sts.

**All tops**

Cont straight until Back matches Fronts to start of shoulder shaping, ending with a WS row.

**Shape shoulder**

Bind (cast) off 4 (5: 7: 6: 6: 7: 8) sts at beg of next 2 (2: 2: 4: 4: 4: 4)

rows, then 5 (6: 8: 5: 7: 7: 7) sts at beg of foll 2 rows.

Bind (cast) off rem 15 (17: 21: 23: 25: 27: 29) sts.

## Sleeves (make 2)

With 3³/₄mm (US size 5/UK No.9) needles, cast on 27 (35: 45: 43: 45: 47: 49) sts.

Starting with a k row, work in stockinette (stocking) stitch as follows:

**Bear's top only**

Work 13 (13: 13) rows.

Starting again with a k row (to reverse RS of work), cont in stockinette (stocking) stitch until Sleeve measures 4³/₄ (6: 6¹/₂)in, 12 (15: 17)cm, ending with a WS row.

**Child's top only**

Dec 1 st at each end of (5ᵗʰ: 3ʳᵈ: 3ʳᵈ: 3ʳᵈ) and every foll 6ᵗʰ row until (37: 39: 41: 43) sts rem.

Work a further (4: 6: 6: 6) rows.

Starting again with a k row (to reverse RS of work), cont in stockinette (stocking) stitch, shaping sides by inc 1 st at each end of (3ʳᵈ: 5ᵗʰ: 5ᵗʰ: 5ᵗʰ) and every foll 6ᵗʰ row to (55: 55: 63: 61) sts, then on every foll (0: 8ᵗʰ: 8ᵗʰ: 8ᵗʰ) row until there are (55: 59: 65: 69) sts. Cont straight until Sleeve measures (9³/₄: 11¹/₂: 13: 14¹/₂)in, (25: 29: 33: 37)cm, ending with a WS row.

**Shape top**

Place markers at both ends of last row to mark top of sleeve seam.

Work a further 8 rows, ending with a WS row.

**All tops**

Bind (cast) off rem 27 (35: 45: 55: 59: 65: 69) sts.

## Ties (make 2)

With 3mm (US size 2–3/UK No.11) needles, cast on 6 sts.

Work in garter stitch until Tie measures 13³/₄ (15³/₄: 17³/₄: 23¹/₂: 25¹/₂: 27¹/₂: 29¹/₂)in, 35 (40: 45: 60: 65: 70: 75)cm.

Bind (cast) off.

## Making up

Join shoulder seams. Matching center of bound-off (cast-off) edge of Sleeves to shoulder seams, sew Sleeves to Back and Fronts. Join side and sleeve seams, reversing sleeve seam for first 13 (13: 13: 21: 21: 21: 21) rows and leaving an opening in one side seam for Tie. Fold 1¹/₂ (1¹/₂: 1¹/₂: 2¹/₄: 2¹/₄: 2¹/₄: 2¹/₄)in, 4 (4: 4: 6: 6: 6: 6)cm, cuff to RS.

**Crochet edging**

With 3mm (US size D3/UK No.11) crochet hook and Lurex

Shimmer, attach yarn at base of left side seam and work 1 round of single (double) crochet around entire hem, front opening and neck edge, working a multiple of 3 sts and ending with a slip stitch into first st.

**NEXT ROUND:** Chain 1 (does NOT count as st), *1 single (double) crochet into each of next 2 single (double) crochet, chain 3, slip stitch to top of last single (double) crochet worked; rep from * to end, slip stitch to first st.

Fasten off.

Work Crochet Edging around lower edge of Sleeves in same way. Sew cast-on edges of Ties in position behind Edging and level with first straight section of front opening edge.

# peruvian hat, scarf, and bag

This jolly hat, scarf, and bag are perfect for adventuresome tots.
Knitted in soft 4-ply wool, the cheery colors will brighten winter days.

## Sizes and finished knitted measurements

| | Child | | | |
|---|---|---|---|---|
| To fit age | 2–3 | | | yrs |
| **Hat** | | | | |
| Width around head | 18 | | | in |
| | 46 | | | cm |
| **Scarf** | | | | |
| Actual measurement | 7¹/₂ | × | 45¹/₄ | in |
| | 19 | × | 115 | cm |
| **Bag** | | | | |
| Actual measurement | 6¹/₂ | × | 6¹/₂ | in |
| | 17 | × | 17 | cm |

## Materials

**YARN:** 3 x 50g (1³/₄oz) balls of Rowan 4-ply Soft in A (pink), and
1 ball in each of B (cream), C (camel), D (lime), E (turquoise), F
(lilac) and G (cherry)

**KNITTING NEEDLES:** Pair each of 2³/₄mm (US size 2/UK No.12) and
3¹/₄mm (US size 3/UK No.10) needles

**BUTTONS:** 3 for Bag

## Abbreviations

See page 93.

## Stitch gauge/tension

30 sts and 34 rows to 4in, 10cm, measured over fairisle pattern,
28 sts and 36 rows to 4in, 10cm, measured over stockinette
(stocking) stitch on 3¹/₄mm (US size 3/UK No.10) needles.

## Note

When working from charts, work odd numbered rows as knit rows,
reading chart from right to left, and even numbered rows as purl
rows, reading chart from left to right. Strand yarn not in use loosely
across WS of work.

## hat

### Earflaps (make 2)

With 3¹/₄mm (US size 3/UK No.10) needles and yarn B, cast on 10
sts.
Joining and breaking off yarns as required, cont as follows:
**ROW 1 (RS):** Using yarn B, k10.
**ROW 2:** Using yarn E, p to end, inc 1 st at each end of row.

**ROW 3:** Using yarn E, k to end, inc 1 st at each end of row. 14 sts.

**ROW 4:** Using yarn A, p to end, inc 1 st at each end of row.

**ROW 5:** Using yarn G, k to end, inc 1 st at each end of row. 18 sts.

**ROW 6:** Using yarn G, p to end, inc 1 st at each end of row.

**ROW 7:** Using yarn B, k to end, inc 1 st at each end of row.

**ROW 8:** Using yarn D, p to end, inc 1 st at each end of row. 24 sts.

**ROW 9:** Using yarn A, knit.

**ROW 10:** Using yarn A, p to end, inc 1 st at each end of row. 26 sts.

**ROW 11:** Using yarn C, knit.

**ROW 12:** Using yarn C, p to end, inc 1 st at each end of row. 28 sts.

**ROW 13:** Using yarn F, knit.

**ROW 14:** Using yarn F, p to end, inc 1 st at each end of row.

Break yarn and leave these 30 sts on a holder.

## Main Section

With 3¼mm (US size 3/UK No.10) needles and yarn A, cast on 16 sts, turn and knit across 30 sts of first Earflap, turn and cast on 38 sts, turn and knit across 30 sts of second Earflap, turn and cast on 16 sts. 130 sts.

Starting with a p row and joining and breaking off yarns as required, cont in stockinette (stocking) stitch as follows:-
Using yarn A, work 1 row.
Using yarn B, work 1 row.
Using yarn E, work 2 rows.
Using yarn F, work 2 rows.
Using yarn G, work 1 row.
Using yarn A, work 2 rows.
Using yarn D, work 2 rows.
Using yarn C, work 2 rows.
Using yarn A, work 1 row.

Using yarn F, work 2 rows.
Using yarn G, work 1 row.
**NEXT ROW (RS):** Using yarn A, k9, *M1, k8; rep from * to last 9 sts, M1, k9. 145 sts.
Using yarn A, work 1 row.
Repeating the 24 patt sts 6 times across rows and working edge st as indicated, work 21 rows in patt from chart A, ending with a RS row.
Using yarn E, work 2 rows.

### Shape crown

**ROW 1 (WS):** Using yarn F, p2, *p2tog, p3; rep

from * to last 3 sts, p2tog, p1. 116 sts.
Using yarn A, work 1 row.
Using yarn C, work 1 row.
Using yarn F, work 2 rows.
Using yarn G, work 1 row.
**ROW 7:** Using yarn E, p1, *p2tog, p2; rep from * to last 3 sts, p2tog, p1. 87 sts.
Using yarn A, work 2 rows.
Using yarn D, work 1 row.
Using yarn B, work 2 rows.
Using yarn C, work 2 rows.
**ROW 15:** Using yarn B, *p1, p2tog; rep from

# hat

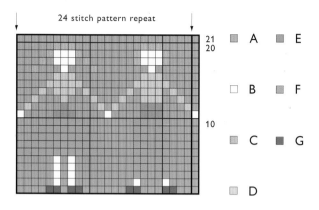

21
20

10

- ■ A   ■ E
- □ B   ■ F
- ■ C   ■ G
- ■ D

* to end. 58 sts.

Using yarn E, work 2 rows.

Using yarn A, work 1 row.

Using yarn F, work 2 rows.

**ROW 21:** Using yarn D, (p2tog) to end. 29 sts.

Using yarn E, work 1 row.

Using yarn A, work 2 rows.

**ROW 25:** Using yarn B, p1, (p2tog) 14 times. 15 sts.

Using yarn F, work 2 rows.

Using yarn B, work 1 row.

Using yarn E, work 1 row.

Using yarn A, work 2 rows.

Break yarn and thread through rem 15 sts. Pull up tight and fasten off securely.

## Lower Edging

With RS facing, 2³/₄mm (US size 2/UK No.12) needles and yarn E, pick up and knit 16 sts along first cast-on edge of Main Section, 54 sts around first Earflap, 38 sts along next cast-on edge, 54 sts around second Earflap, then 16 sts along final cast-on edge. 178 sts.

Knit 2 rows.

Bind (cast) off knitwise (on WS).

## Making up

Join back seam. Using yarn F, make two twisted cords, each 2in, 5cm, long. Using all colors, make two pompons 1¹/₂in, 4cm, diameter. Attach a pompon to one end of each cord and then attach other ends of cords to lower edge of Earflaps.

# bag and scarf

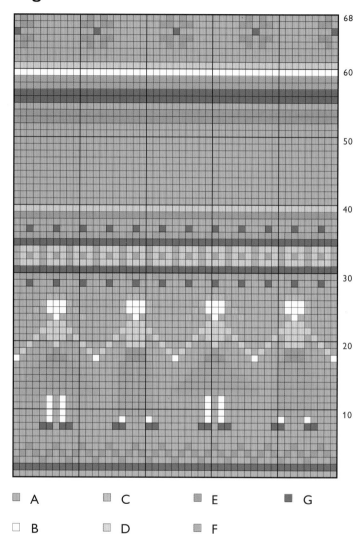

68

60

50

40

30

20

10

- ■ A   ■ C   ■ E   ■ G
- □ B   ■ D   ■ F

# scarf

With 2³/₄mm (US size 2/UK No.12) needles and yarn A, cast on 53 sts.

Work in garter stitch for 5 rows, ending with a WS row.

Change to 3¹/₄mm (US size 3/UK No.10) needles.

**NEXT ROW (RS):** Using yarn A k2, work next 49 sts as row 1 of chart

B, using yarn A k2.

**NEXT ROW:** Using yarn A k2, work next 49 sts as row 2 of chart B, using yarn A k2.

These 2 rows set position of chart B with first and last 2 sts of every row worked as k sts using yarn A.

Cont as set until all 68 rows of chart B have been completed.

Break off contrasts and cont using yarn A only.

**NEXT ROW (RS):** Knit.

**NEXT ROW:** K2, p to last 2 sts, k2.

Rep last 2 rows until Scarf measures 37$^{1}$/$_{2}$in, 95cm, ending with a WS row.

Now reading chart in reverse (by working even numbered rows as k rows and odd numbered rows as p rows) and from top to bottom, cont as follows:

**NEXT ROW (RS):** Using yarn A k2, work next 49 sts as row 68 of chart B, using yarn A k2.

**NEXT ROW:** Using yarn A k2, work next 49 sts as row 67 of chart B, using yarn A k2.

These 2 rows set position of chart B with first and last 2 sts of every row worked as k sts using yarn A.

Cont as set until all 68 rows of chart B have been completed.

Break off contrasts and cont using yarn A only.

Change to 2$^{3}$/$_{4}$mm (US size 2/UK No.12) needles.

Work in garter stitch for 5 rows.

Bind (cast) off knitwise (on WS).

## Making up

Using all colors make four pompons 1$^{1}$/$_{2}$in, 4cm, diameter and attach one pompon to each corner of Scarf.

### Embroidery

Using photograph as a guide, embroider a row of flowers across wide band of yarn A near ends, and separate flowers at random over center section. For each flowerhead, embroider 5 lazy daisy stitches radiating out from one point using yarn G. To form a stem and leaves, embroider a stem stitch and two individual lazy daisy stitches in yarn D.

## *bag*
## Front

With 3$^{1}$/$_{4}$mm (US size 3/UK No.10) needles and yarn A, cast on 49 sts.

Starting with a k row, work in stockinette (stocking) stitch for

2 rows, ending with a WS row.

Now work rows 1 to 60 of chart B, ending with a WS row.**

Bind (cast) off.

## Back

Work as given for Front to **.

Break off all contrasts and cont using yarn A only.

Work in garter stitch for 10 rows.

**NEXT ROW (RS):** K3, k2tog, yfwd, k18, k2tog, yfwd, k19, yfwd, k2tog, k3.

Work a further 4 rows in garter stitch.

Bind (cast) off knitwise (on WS).

## Strap

With 2$^{3}$/$_{4}$mm (US size 2/UK No.12) needles and yarn A, cast on 5 sts.

Work in garter stitch until strap measures 23$^{1}$/$_{2}$in, 60cm.

Bind (cast) off.

## Making up

Sew Front and Back together along cast-on and row end edges, enclosing ends of Strap in top of seam. Fold garter stitch section of Back over onto Front to form flap and attach buttons to Front to correspond with buttonholes.

### Embroidery

Using photograph as a guide, embroider a row of flowers across wide band of yarn A. For each flowerhead, embroider 5 lazy daisy stitches radiating out from one point using yarn G. To form a stem and leaves, embroider a stem stitch and two individual lazy daisy stitches in yarn D.

# patchwork blanket and cushion

Make bedtime special for your little cherub with this pretty blanket and cushion featuring teddies, rocking horses, dolls, and dollhouses—images that can be woven into bedtime stories.

## Sizes and finished knitted measurements

### Blanket

| | | | | |
|---|---|---|---|---|
| Actual measurement | $28^3/4$ | x | $36^1/4$ | in |
| | 73 | x | 92 | cm |

### Cushion

| | | | | |
|---|---|---|---|---|
| Actual measurement | $17^3/4$ | x | $15^3/4$ | in |
| | 45 | x | 40 | cm |

## Materials

### Blanket

**YARN:** 12 x 50g ($1^3/4$oz) balls of Rowan Handknit DK Cotton in A (ecru), 2 balls in each of B (light brown), C (light blue), D (pink), E (yellow), F (mid blue) and G (lavender), and 1 ball in each of H (beige) and J (black)

**KNITTING NEEDLES:** Pair of 4mm (US size 6/UK No.8) needles

### Cushion

**YARN:** 5 x 50g ($1^3/4$oz) balls of Rowan Handknit DK Cotton in A (ecru), 1 ball in each of B (light brown), C (light blue), D (pink), E (light green), F (mid-blue) and G (lavender), and oddments of H (beige) and J (black)

**KNITTING NEEDLES:** Pair of 4mm (US size 6/UK No.8) needles

**CUSHION PAD:** $17^3/4$in x $15^3/4$in, 45cm x 40cm, cushion pad

## Abbreviations

See page 93.

## Stitch gauge/tension

20 sts and 28 rows to 4in, 10cm, measured over stockinette (stocking) stitch on 4mm (US size 6/UK No.8) needles.

## Note

When working from charts, work odd numbered rows as knit rows, reading chart from right to left, and even numbered rows as purl rows, reading chart from left to right. Use a separate ball of yarn for each block of color, twisting colors together where they meet to avoid holes forming.

## Stripe Panel

Starting with a k row, work in stockinette (stocking) stitch using colors as follows:

**ROWS 1 AND 2:** Using yarn C.
**ROWS 3 AND 4:** Using yarn F.
**ROWS 5 AND 6:** Using yarn E.
**ROWS 7 AND 8:** Using yarn G.
**ROWS 9 AND 10:** Using yarn D.
**ROWS 11 AND 12:** Using yarn B.
**ROWS 13 AND 14:** Using yarn A.
**ROWS 15 TO 28:** As rows 1 to 14.
**ROWS 29 TO 32:** As rows 1 to 4.
These 32 rows form Stripe Panel.

## Blanket

With 4mm (US size 6/UK No.8) needles and yarn A, cast on 145 sts.
Work in garter stitch for 5 rows, ending with a WS row.
**ROW 6 (RS):** Using yarn A k5, work next 23 sts as row 1 of Rocking Horse Panel, using yarn A k5, work next 23 sts as row 1 of Stripe Panel, using yarn A k5, work next 23 sts as row 1 of House Panel, using yarn A k5, work next 23 sts as row 1 of Stripe Panel, using yarn A k5, work next 23 sts as row 1 of Teddy Panel, using yarn A k5.

**ROW 7:** Using yarn A k5, work next 23 sts as row 2 of Teddy Panel, using yarn A k5, work next 23 sts as row 2 of Stripe Panel, using yarn A k5, work next 23 sts as row 2 of House Panel, using yarn A k5, work next 23 sts as row 2 of Stripe Panel, using yarn A k5, work next 23 sts as row 2 of Rocking Horse Panel, using yarn A k5.
These 2 rows set position of panels.
Cont as set until all 32 rows of panels have been completed.
Using yarn A, work in garter stitch for 6 rows, ending with a WS row.
**ROW 44 (RS):** Using yarn A k5, work next 23 sts as row 1 of Stripe Panel, using yarn A k5, work next 23 sts as row 1 of Doll Panel, using yarn A k5, work next 23 sts as row 1 of Stripe Panel, using yarn A k5, work next 23 sts as row 1 of Rocking Horse Panel, using yarn A k5, work next 23 sts as row 1 of Stripe Panel, using yarn A k5.
**ROW 45:** Using yarn A k5, work next 23 sts as row 2 of Stripe Panel, using yarn A k5, work next 23 sts as row 2 of Rocking Horse Panel, using yarn A k5, work next 23 sts as row 2 of Stripe Panel, using yarn A k5, work next 23 sts as row 2 of Doll Panel, using yarn A k5, work next 23 sts as row 2 of Stripe Panel, using yarn A k5.
These 2 rows set position of panels.
Cont as set until all 32 rows of panels have been completed.
Using yarn A, work in garter stitch for 6 rows, ending with a WS row.
**ROW 82 (RS):** Using yarn A k5, work next 23 sts as row 1 of House Panel, using yarn A k5, work next 23 sts as row 1 of Stripe Panel, using yarn A k5, work next 23 sts as row 1 of Teddy Panel, using yarn A k5, work next 23 sts as row 1 of Stripe Panel, using yarn A k5, work next 23 sts as row 1 of Doll Panel, using yarn A k5.
**ROW 83:** Using yarn A k5, work next 23 sts as row 2 of Doll Panel, using yarn A k5, work next 23 sts as row 2 of Stripe Panel, using yarn A k5, work next 23 sts as row 2 of Teddy Panel, using yarn A k5, work next 23 sts as row 2 of Stripe Panel, using yarn A k5, work next 23 sts as row 2 of House Panel, using yarn A k5.
These 2 rows set position of panels.
Cont as set until all 32 rows of panels have been completed.
Using yarn A, work in garter stitch for 6 rows, ending with a WS row.
**ROW 120 (RS):** Using yarn A k5, work next 23 sts as row 1 of Stripe Panel, using yarn A k5, work next 23 sts as row 1 of Rocking Horse Panel, using yarn A k5, work next 23 sts as row 1 of Stripe Panel, using yarn A k5, work next 23 sts as row 1 of House Panel, using yarn A k5, work next 23 sts as row 1 of Stripe Panel, using yarn A k5.
**ROW 121:** Using yarn A k5, work next 23 sts as row 2 of Stripe Panel, using yarn A k5, work next 23 sts as row 2 of House Panel, using yarn A k5, work next 23 sts as row 2 of Stripe Panel, using yarn A

## doll panel

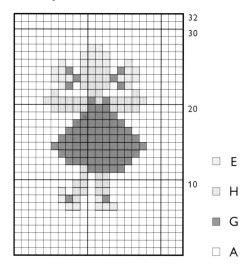

- ☐ E
- ☐ H
- ■ G
- ☐ A

## house panel

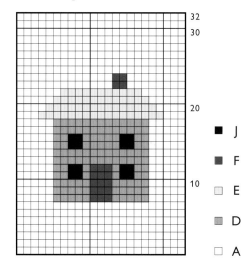

- ■ J
- ■ F
- ☐ E
- ■ D
- ☐ A

k5, work next 23 sts as row 2 of Rocking Horse Panel, using yarn A k5, work next 23 sts as row 2 of Stripe Panel, using yarn A k5.
These 2 rows set position of panels.
Cont as set until all 32 rows of panels have been completed.
Using yarn A, work in garter stitch for 6 rows, ending with a WS row.

**ROW 158 (RS):** Using yarn A k5, work next 23 sts as row 1 of Teddy Panel, using yarn A k5, work next 23 sts as row 1 of Stripe Panel, using yarn A k5, work next 23 sts as row 1 of Doll Panel, using yarn A k5, work next 23 sts as row 1 of Stripe Panel, using yarn A k5, work next 23 sts as row 1 of Rocking Horse Panel, using yarn A k5.

**ROW 159:** Using yarn A k5, work next 23 sts as row 2 of Rocking Horse Panel, using yarn A k5, work next 23 sts as row 2 of Stripe Panel, using yarn A k5, work next 23 sts as row 2 of Doll Panel, using yarn A k5, work next 23 sts as row 2 of Stripe Panel, using yarn A k5, work next 23 sts as row 2 of Teddy Panel, using yarn A k5.

These 2 rows set position of panels.

Cont as set until all 32 rows of panels have been completed.

Using yarn A, work in garter stitch for 6 rows, ending with a WS row.

**ROW 196 (RS):** Using yarn A k5, work next 23 sts as row 1 of Stripe Panel, using yarn A k5, work next 23 sts as row 1 of House Panel, using yarn A k5, work next 23 sts as row 1 of Stripe Panel, using yarn A k5, work next 23 sts as row 1 of Teddy Panel, using yarn A k5, work next 23 sts as row 1 of Stripe Panel, using yarn A k5.

**ROW 197:** Using yarn A k5, work next 23 sts as row 2 of Stripe Panel, using yarn A k5, work next 23 sts as row 2 of Teddy Panel, using yarn A k5, work next 23 sts as row 2 of Stripe Panel, using yarn A k5, work next 23 sts as row 2 of House Panel, using yarn A k5, work next 23 sts as row 2 of Stripe Panel, using yarn A k5.

These 2 rows set position of panels.

Cont as set until all 32 rows of panels have been completed.

Using yarn A, work in garter stitch for 6 rows, ending with a WS row.

**ROW 234 (RS):** Using yarn A k5, work next 23 sts as row 1 of Doll Panel, using yarn A k5, work next 23 sts as row 1 of Stripe Panel, using yarn A k5, work next 23 sts as row 1 of Rocking Horse Panel, using yarn A k5, work next 23 sts as row 1 of Stripe Panel, using yarn A k5, work next 23 sts as row 1 of House Panel, using yarn A k5.

**ROW 235:** Using yarn A k5, work next 23 sts as row 2 of House Panel, using yarn A k5, work next 23 sts as row 2 of Stripe Panel, using yarn A k5, work next 23 sts as row 2 of Rocking Horse Panel, using yarn A k5, work next 23 sts as row 2 of Stripe Panel, using yarn A k5, work next 23 sts as row 2 of Doll Panel, using yarn A k5.

These 2 rows set position of panels.

Cont as set until all 32 rows of panels have been completed.

Using yarn A, work in garter stitch for 6 rows, ending with a WS row. Bind (cast) off.

## rocking horse panel

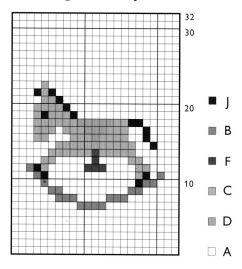

- ■ J
- ■ B
- ■ F
- ■ C
- ■ D
- □ A

## teddy panel

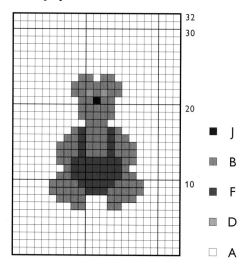

- ■ J
- ■ B
- ■ F
- ■ D
- □ A

**Embroidery**

Using yarn C, embroider french knot buttons onto Teddy's trousers, and using yarn J embroider Teddy's mouth. Using yarn F, embroider french knot eyes onto Doll and using yarn D embroider Doll's mouth.

## Cushion Sides (make 2)

With 4mm (US size 6/UK No.8) needles and yarn A, cast on 89 sts. Work in garter stitch for 5 rows, ending with a WS row.

**ROW 6 (RS):** Using yarn A k5, work next 23 sts as row 1 of Rocking Horse Panel, using yarn A k5, work next 23 sts as row 1 of Stripe Panel, using yarn A k5, work next 23 sts as row 1 of House Panel, using yarn A k5.

**ROW 7:** Using yarn A k5, work next 23 sts as row 2 of House Panel, using yarn A k5, work next 23 sts as row 2 of Stripe Panel, using yarn A k5, work next 23 sts as row 2 of Rocking Horse Panel, using yarn A k5.

These 2 rows set position of panels.

Cont as set until all 32 rows of panels have been completed.

Using yarn A, work in garter stitch for 6 rows, ending with a WS row.

**ROW 44 (RS):** Using yarn A k5, work next 23 sts as row 1 of Stripe Panel, using yarn A k5, work next 23 sts as row 1 of Teddy Panel, using yarn A k5, work next 23 sts as row 1 of Stripe Panel, using yarn A k5.

**ROW 45:** Using yarn A k5, work next 23 sts as row 2 of Stripe Panel, using yarn A k5, work next 23 sts as row 2 of Teddy Panel, using yarn A k5, work next 23 sts as row 2 of Stripe Panel, using yarn A k5.

These 2 rows set position of panels.

Cont as set until all 32 rows of panels have been completed.

Using yarn A, work in garter stitch for 6 rows, ending with a WS row.

**ROW 82 (RS):** Using yarn A k5, work next 23 sts as row 1 of Doll Panel, using yarn A k5, work next 23 sts as row 1 of Stripe Panel, using yarn A k5, work next 23 sts as row 1 of Rocking Horse Panel, using yarn A k5.

**ROW 83:** Using yarn A k5, work next 23 sts as row 2 of Rocking Horse Panel, using yarn A k5, work next 23 sts as row 2 of Stripe Panel, using yarn A k5, work next 23 sts as row 2 of Doll Panel, using yarn A k5.

These 2 rows set position of panels.

Cont as set until all 32 rows of panels have been completed.

Using yarn A, work in garter stitch for 6 rows, ending with a WS row. Bind (cast) off.

**Embroidery**

Using yarn C, embroider french knot buttons onto Teddy's trousers, and using yarn J embroider Teddy's mouth. Using yarn F, embroider french knot eyes onto Doll and using yarn D embroider Doll's mouth.

Join Sides together along 3 edges. Insert cushion pad and close fourth Side.

# bear backpack

This tweed bear bag will be loved by kids of all ages, and you will fall for it too.
Knit it in a chunky, flecked wool and alpaca yarn.

## Sizes and finished knitted measurements

|  | Bear |  |
| --- | --- | --- |
| Height of bag | 11³/₄ | in |
|  | 30 | cm |
| Width of base | 9¹/₂ | in |
|  | 25 | cm |

## Materials

**YARN:** 3 x 100g (3¹/₂oz) balls of Jaeger Shetland Aran in A (beige tweed) and 1 ball in B (light brown)
Scrap of dark brown yarn for embroidery
**KNITTING NEEDLES:** Pair each of 3³/₄mm (US size 5/UK No.9) needles
**SUNDRIES:** Pair of toy safety-locking eyes, washable toy filling

## Abbreviations

See page 93.

## Stitch gauge/tension

22 sts and 28 rows to 4in, 10cm, measured over stockinette (stocking) stitch on 3³/₄mm (US size 5/UK No.9) needles.

## Left Side Head

With 3³/₄mm (US size 5/UK No.9) needles and yarn A, cast on 7 sts.
Starting with a k row, work in stockinette (stocking) stitch throughout as follows:
**ROW 1 (RS):** Inc once in each of first 6 sts, k1. 13 sts.
**ROW 2:** (P1, inc purlwise in next st) 6 times, p1. 19 sts.
Inc 1 st at beg (back head edge) of next and foll 4th row and at same time inc 1 st at end (chin edge) of next and every foll alt row. 25 sts.

Inc 1 st at chin edge of next 12 rows and at same time inc 1 st at back edge of 4th and foll 3 alt rows. 41 sts.
Work 1 row, ending with a WS row.
Inc 1 st at back edge of next row. 42 sts.
Work 9 rows, ending with a RS row.
Place marker at end of last row to mark nose.
Bind (cast) off 6 sts at beg of next and foll alt row and at same time dec 1 st at back edge of 2nd of these rows. 29 sts.
Dec 1 st at back edge of next and foll alt row, then on foll 5 rows and at same time dec 1 st at nose edge of every row.
Bind (cast) off rem 14 sts.

## Right Side Head

Work as for Left Side Head, but starting with a p row and reading p for k and vice versa.

## Head Gusset

With 3³/₄mm (US size 5/UK No.9) needles and yarn A, cast on 3 sts.
Starting with a k row, work in stockinette (stocking) stitch throughout as follows:
**ROW 1 (RS):** Inc once in each st. 6 sts.
Work 7 rows.
Inc 1 st at each end of next and foll 8th row, then on every foll 4th row until there are 26 sts.
Work 11 rows, ending with a WS row.
Dec 1 st at each end of next and every foll 4th row to 18 sts, then on foll 2 alt rows, then on every foll 4th row to 10 sts, then on foll 3 alt rows, then on foll row.
**NEXT ROW (RS):** K2tog and fasten off.

## Ears (make 4)

With 3³/₄mm (US size 5/UK No.9) needles and yarn A, cast on 9 sts.

Starting with a k row, work in stockinette (stocking) stitch throughout as follows:

**ROW 1 (RS):** Inc once in each st. 18 sts.

Work 3 rows.

Dec 1 st at each end of next and foll 2 alt rows, then on 3 rows.

Bind (cast) off rem 6 sts.

Matching cast-on edges and fasten-off point of Gusset to marker at nose, sew Gusset to Side Head pieces. Sew chin seam below markers, leaving an opening to insert toy filling. Attach eyes as in photograph. Insert toy filling so head is fairly softly filled, then close opening in chin seam. Sew pairs of Ears together, leaving cast-on edge open. Turn RS out and slipstitch cast-on edges closed. Position ears on head as in photograph and stitch in place. Embroider nose and mouth as in photograph.

## Legs (make 2)

With 3³/₄mm (US size 5/UK No.9) needles and yarn A, cast on 41 sts.

Starting with a k row, work in stockinette (stocking) stitch throughout as follows:

Dec 1 st at each end of 3ʳᵈ and foll alt row, then on foll row. 35 sts.

**NEXT ROW (RS):** K2tog, k15, M1, k1, M1, k15, k2tog. 35 sts.

Dec 1 st at each end of next row. 33 sts.

Bind (cast) off 5 sts at beg of next 2 rows. 23 sts.

Work 4 rows.

Inc 1 st at each end of next and foll 2 alt rows. 29 sts.

Work 1 row.

**NEXT ROW (RS):** Inc in first st, k13, M1, k1, M1, k13, inc in last st. 33 sts.

Work 3 rows.

Inc 1 st at each end of next and every foll 4ᵗʰ row until there are 39 sts.

Work 9 rows.

Place marker on center st of last row.

**NEXT ROW (RS):** K2tog, k to within 1 st of marked center st, sl 1, k2tog, psso, k to last 2 sts, k2tog.

Work 1 row.

Rep last 2 rows 3 times more.

Bind (cast) off rem 23 sts.

## Soles (make 2)

With 3³/₄mm (US size 5/UK No.9) needles and yarn B, cast on 6 sts.
Starting with a p row, work in reverse stockinette (stocking) stitch throughout as follows:
Work 1 row.
Inc 1 st at each end of next 2 rows, then on foll alt row. 12 sts.
Work 11 rows, ending with a WS row.
Dec 1 st at each end of next and foll 3ʳᵈ row, then on foll alt row, ending with a WS row.
Bind (cast) off rem 6 sts.

Join front seam of each Leg, leaving bound-off (cast-off) edge open. Matching center of cast-on edge of Sole to front leg seam, sew Sole to cast-on edge of foot section. Insert toy filling so Leg is softly filled and fold top of Leg so that front seam is positioned centrally along Leg. Stitch upper edge closed.

## Arms (make 2)

With 3³/₄mm (US size 5/UK No.9) needles and yarn A, cast on 11 sts.
Starting with a k row, work in stockinette (stocking) stitch throughout as follows:
Work 1 row.
Place marker on center st of last row.
**NEXT ROW (WS):** Inc in first st, p to marked st, M1, p marked st, M1, p to last st, inc in last st. 15 sts.
**NEXT ROW:** Inc in first st, k to marked st, M1, k marked st, M1, k to last st, inc in last st. 19 sts.
**NEXT ROW:** Inc in first st, p to marked st, M1, p marked st, M1, p to last st, inc in last st. 23 sts.
**NEXT ROW:** K to marked st, M1, k marked st, M1, k to end. 25 sts.
Work 1 row.
Rep last 2 rows once more. 27 sts.
Dec 1 st at each end of next and foll 2 alt rows. 21 sts.
Work 7 rows, ending with a WS row.
Inc 1 st at each end of next and foll 9 alt rows. 41 sts.
Work 1 row.
**NEXT ROW (RS):** K to within 1 st of marked st, sl 1, k2tog, psso, k to end. 39 sts.
Work 3 rows.
**NEXT ROW:** K to within 1 st of marked st, sl 1, k2tog, psso, k to end. 37 sts.
Work 1 row.

**NEXT ROW:** K2tog, k to within 1 st of marked st, sl 1, k2tog, psso, k to last 2 sts, k2tog. 33 sts.
Work 1 row.
Rep last 2 rows twice more.
Bind (cast) off rem 25 sts.

## Paws (make 2)

With 3³/₄mm (US size 5/UK No.9) needles and yarn B, cast on 2 sts.
Starting with a p row, work in reverse stockinette (stocking) stitch throughout as follows:
Work 1 row.
Inc 1 st at each end of next 3 rows. 8 sts.
Work 5 rows, ending with a RS row.
Dec 1 st at each end of next 3 rows, ending with a WS row.
Bind (cast) off rem 2 sts.

Join front seam of each Arm, leaving bound-off (cast-off) edge open. Insert toy filling so Arm is softly filled and stitch upper edge closed. Position Paw inside hand section as in photograph and stitch in place.

## Main Bag Section

With 3³/₄mm (US size 5/UK No.9) needles and yarn A, cast on 80 sts.
Starting with a k row, work in stockinette (stocking) stitch throughout as follows:
Work 5 rows, ending with a RS row.
**ROW 6 (WS):** P8, yrn, p2tog, p7, yrn, p2tog, p22, p2tog tbl, yrn, p7, p2tog tbl, yrn, p8.
Work a further 7 rows, ending with a RS row.
**ROW 14 (WS):** Knit (to form fold line).
Starting with a k row, work in stockinette (stocking) stitch throughout as follows:
Work 7 rows.
**ROW 22 (WS):** As row 6.
Cont straight until work measures 11³/₄in, 30cm, from fold line row, ending with a WS row.
Bind (cast) off 13 sts at beg of next 2 rows. 54 sts.
Cont straight until work measures 16¹/₂in, 42cm, from fold line row, ending with a WS row.
Cast on 13 sts at beg of next 2 rows. 80 sts.
Cont straight until work measures 27in, 69cm, from fold line row, ending with a WS row.
**FRONT EYELET ROW (RS):** K8, yfwd, k2tog, k7, (yfwd, k2tog, k5) twice, yfwd, k2tog, k14, k2tog tbl, yfwd, (k5, K2tog tbl, yfwd) twice, k7, K2tog tbl, yfwd, k8.
Work a further 7 rows, ending with a WS row.
**NEXT ROW (RS):** Purl (to form fold line).
Starting with a k row, work in stockinette (stocking) stitch throughout as follows:
Work 7 rows, ending with a WS row.
Rep the front eyelet row once more.
Work a further 5 rows.
Bind (cast) off.
Matching cast-on and bound-off (cast-off) edges, sew side seams.
Fold cast-on and bound-off (cast-off) edges to inside along fold line rows and stitch in place.

## Shoulder Straps (make 2)

With 3³/₄mm (US size 5/UK No.9) needles and yarn A, cast on 16 sts.
Starting with a k row, work in stockinette (stocking) stitch until Strap measures 15in, 38cm.
Bind (cast) off.

Fold Strap in half and stitch along long edge to form long thin tube. Turn RS out. Sew one end of each Strap to outside of back of main Section, positioning Straps between central eyelet holes.

Fold Bag so that cast-on and bound-off (cast-off) sts at "base" of Bag match row end edges of shorter center section. Inserting free end of each Strap into seam at back corners, sew base gusset seams.

## Flap (make 2)

With 3³/₄mm (US size 5/UK No.9) needles and yarn A, cast on 27 sts.
Starting with a k row, work in stockinette (stocking) stitch throughout as follows:
Work 6 rows, ending with a WS row.
Inc 1 st at each end of next and every foll 6ᵗʰ row until there are 33 sts.
Work 15 rows, ending with a WS row.
Dec 1 st at each end of next and foll 2 alt rows, then on foll 5 rows.
Bind (cast) off rem 17 sts.

Sew Flaps together, leaving cast-on edges open. Turn RS out and stitch cast-on edges together. Positioning cast-on edge level with eyelets, sew this edge of Flap to outside of back of Bag Section. Fold Flap over to front of bag, flatten Head slightly and sew to Flap as in photograph. Make a twisted cord 39¹/₂in, 100cm, long and, positioning center of cord at center of back of bag, on outside, thread cord in and out of eyelet holes around upper edge, leaving ends free at center front. Pull up cord to close bag. Sew Legs to base of Bag, and Arms to sides of Bag as in photograph.

# *christmas stocking*

Knit these matching Christmas stockings and add to the fun and excitement of Christmas Eve—teddy and child alike will look forward to seeing what Santa brings.

## Sizes and finished knitted measurements

|  | Bear | Child |  |
|---|---|---|---|
| Height | 13³/₄ | 24 | in |
|  | 35 | 61 | cm |
| Length of foot | 11¹/₂ | 15¹/₄ | in |
|  | 29 | 39 | cm |

## Materials

**YARN:** 1 (2) × 50g (1³/₄oz) balls of Rowan Wool Cotton in A (blue), 1 ball in each of B (red), C (camel), D (green), and scrap of E (black) for embroidery

**KNITTING NEEDLES:** Pair of 3³/₄mm (US size 5/UK No.9) needles

**SUNDRIES:** Piece of fabric 23¹/₂ (31¹/₂)in, 60 (80)cm square for lining (optional)

## Abbreviations

See page 93.

## Stitch gauge/tension

24 sts and 32 rows to 4in, 10cm, measured over stockinette (stocking) stitch on 3³/₄mm (US size 5/UK No.9) needles.

## Note

When working from chart, work odd numbered rows as knit rows, reading chart from right to left, and even numbered rows as purl rows, reading chart from left to right.

## First Side

With 3³/₄mm (US size 5/UK No.9) needles, cast on as follows:
0 (7) sts using yarn B, 42 (54) sts using yarn A, (2 sts using yarn B,

2 sts using yarn A) 0 (3) times, 2 sts using yarn B, and 0 (1) st using yarn A. 50 (76) sts.

Starting with a k row and joining in and breaking off colors as required, work in stockinette (stocking) stitch following appropriate chart as follows:

Work 1 row.

Inc 1 st at each end of next 8 (9) rows. 66 (94) sts.

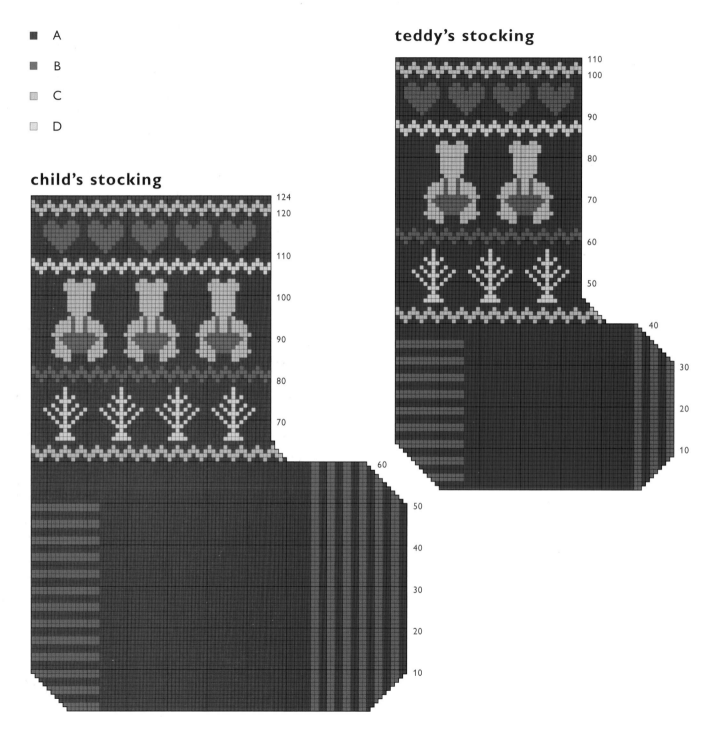

- ■ A
- ■ B
- ■ C
- ■ D

**teddy's stocking**

**child's stocking**

**Bear's stocking only**

Inc 1 st at beg of next row and at same edge of foll 2 rows. 69 sts.

**Both stockings**

Cont straight until chart row 31 (50) has been completed, ending
with a RS (WS) row.

Dec 1 st at end (beg) of next row and at same edge on foll 8 (9)
rows, ending with a WS row. 60 (84) sts.

Bind (cast) off 8 (20) sts at beg of next row. 52 (64) sts.

Dec 1 st at end of next row and at same edge of foll 5 (2) rows,
then on foll 0 (1) alt row. 46 (60) sts.

Cont straight until chart row 104 (124) has been completed, ending
with a WS row.

**Child's stocking only**

Rep chart rows 61 to 124 once more.

**Both stockings**

Break off all contrasts and cont using yarn A only.

**NEXT ROW (RS):** *K1, p1; rep from * to end.

Rep last row 7 times more.

Bind (cast) off in rib.

## Second Side

Work as given for First Side, but reversing design by working odd
numbered rows as p rows, reading chart from right to left, and even
numbered rows as k rows, reading chart from left to right.

## Making up

Sew Sides together, leaving upper edges open. Using yarn A, make a
twisted cord 11³/₄ (13³/₄)in, 30 (35)cm, long and two pompoms 1¹/₄
(1¹/₂)in diameter, 3 (4)cm, diameter using all colors. Attach a pompon
to each end of cord then attach center of cord to back seam just
below upper edge ribbing.

**Embroidery**

Using yarn E and following photograph as a guide, embroider french
knot eyes, satin stitch noses and straight stitch mouths onto bears.

**Optional lining**

Cut out two pieces from lining fabric same size as knitted pieces,
allowing ¹/₂in, 1.2cm, seam allowance along all edges. Sew pieces
together along shaped edges, leaving upper edge open. Fold seam
allowance to WS around upper edge and slip lining inside knitted
sections. Slipstitch upper edge in place.

# *little teddy*

This pocket-sized treasure is created in wonderful cashmere and
extra-fine merino to make a little companion that any child will cherish.

## Sizes and finished knitted measurements

| | | |
|---|---|---|
| Actual height | 5 | in |
| | 13 | cm |

## Materials

**YARN:** 1 x 25g (1oz) ball of Jaeger Cashmina in cream, pink, grey or
camel (this is sufficient for 2 teddies), and oddment in cream, pink or
grey for Scarf

Scrap of brown yarn for embroidery

**KNITTING NEEDLES:** Pair each of 2³/₄mm (US size 2/UK No.12)
needles

**SUNDRIES:** Washable toy filling

## Abbreviations

See page 93.

## Stitch gauge/tension

32 sts and 42 rows to 4in, 10cm, measured over stockinette
(stocking) stitch on 2³/₄mm (US size 2/UK No.12) needles.

## Body (make 2)

With 2³/₄mm (US size 2/UK No.12) needles, cast on 16 sts.
Starting with a k row, work in stockinette (stocking) stitch throughout
as follows:
Work 28 rows, ending with a WS row.

### Shape arm

**NEXT ROW (RS):** K8 and turn, leaving rem sts on a holder.
Cast on 8 sts at beg of next row. 16 sts.
Work a further 7 rows, ending with a RS row.

Bind (cast) off 12 sts at beg of next row.
Break yarn and leave rem 4 sts on a holder.
With RS facing, rejoin yarn to rem 8 sts, cast on 8 sts, k to end. 16 sts.
Work a further 8 rows, ending with a RS row.
**NEXT ROW (WS):** P4, bind (cast) off rem 12 sts.
Break yarn and leave rem 4 sts on a holder.

## Head

With RS facing and 2³/₄mm (US size 2/UK No.12) needles, knit
across first 4 sts of first Body section, and across second set of
4 sts of same Body section, then knit across first 4 sts of second
Body section, then across second set of 4 sts of same Body
section. 16 sts.
Starting with a p row, work in stockinette (stocking) stitch
throughout as follows:
Work 1 row.
**NEXT ROW (RS):** K2, (inc in next st, k1) 6 times, k2. 22 sts.
Work 1 row.
**NEXT ROW:** Inc in first st, (k4, inc in next st) 3 times, k5, inc in last st.
27 sts.
**NEXT ROW:** Inc in first st, p to last st, inc in last st. 29 sts.
**NEXT ROW:** Inc in first st, (k6, inc in next st) twice, k5, inc in next st,
k7, inc in last st. 34 sts.
Work 1 row.
Bind (cast) off 3 sts at beg of next 2 rows. 28 sts.
Dec 1 st at each end of next 2 rows. 24 sts.
**NEXT ROW (RS):** K2tog, k2, sl 1, k1, psso, k5, k2tog, k5, k2tog, k2, k2tog.
19 sts.
Work 1 row.
**NEXT ROW (RS):** K2tog, k1, sl 1, k1, psso, k3, k2tog, k4, k2tog, k1,

k2tog. 14 sts.

Work 1 row.

Dec 1 st at each end of next and foll alt row. 10 sts.

Work 3 rows.

Dec 1 st at each end of next and foll 4<sup>th</sup> row, then on foll 2 alt rows. 2 sts.

Work 1 row.

**NEXT ROW (RS):** K2tog and fasten off.

## Ears (make 4)

With 2³/₄mm (US size 2/UK No.12) needles, cast on 4 sts.

**ROW 1 (RS):** Inc once in each st to end. 8 sts.

**ROW 2:** Purl.

**ROW 3:** Knit.

**ROWS 4 AND 5:** As rows 2 and 3.

Bind (cast) off.

## Scarf

With 2³/₄mm (US size 2/UK No.12) needles, cast on 5 sts.

Work in garter stitch until Scarf measures 9in, 23cm.

Bind (cast) off.

## Making up

RS facing, sew pairs of Ears together leaving lower edge open. Turn RS out and sew Ears to Head as in photograph. Join center front and back seams of Body and Head, leaving lower 2¹/₄in, 6cm, free to form legs and an opening to insert filling. Join leg and foot seams. Join arm and hand seams. Matching fasten-off point of Head to top of seam, sew remaining seams of Head section.

### Embroidery

Using brown yarn and following the photograph as a guide, embroider french knot eyes, satin stitch nose and straight stitch mouth onto Head.

# useful information

Below you will find some useful information about knitting and simple guidelines
to help ensure that your garments turn out perfectly every time.

## Gauge (tension)

Obtaining the correct gauge (tension) is perhaps the single factor that can make the difference between a successful garment and a disastrous one. It controls both the shape and size of an article, so any variation can distort the look of the finished garment.

I recommend that you knit a square in pattern and/or stockinette (stocking) stitch (depending on the pattern instructions) of perhaps 5–10 more stitches and 5–10 more rows than those given in the tension note. If you have too many stitches to 4in (10cm) try again using thicker needles; if you have too few stitches to 4in (10cm) try again using finer needles. Once you have achieved the correct gauge (tension) your garment will be knitted to the measurements indicated in the size diagram shown at the beginning of the pattern.

## Chart note

Many of the patterns in the book are worked from charts. Each square on a chart represents a stitch and each line of squares a row of knitting. Each color used is given a different symbol or letter and these are shown in the materials section, or in the key alongside the chart of each pattern.

When working from the charts, read odd rows (k) from right to left and even rows (p) from left to right, unless otherwise stated.

## Knitting with color

There are two main methods of working color into a knitted fabric: intarsia and Fair Isle techniques. The first method produces a single thickness of fabric and is usually used where a color is only required in a particular area of a row and does not form a repeating pattern across the row, as in the Fair Isle technique.

### Intarsia

The simplest way to do this is to cut short lengths of yarn for each motif or block of color used in a row. Joining in the various colors at the appropriate point on the row, link one color to the next by twisting them around each other where they meet on the wrong side. All ends can then either be darned along the color join lines as each motif is completed, or "knitted in" to the fabric of the knitting as each color is worked into the pattern. This is done in much the same way as "weaving-in" yarns when working the Fair Isle technique and does save time darning-in ends. It is essential that the tension is noted for intarsia as this may vary from the stockinette (stocking) stitch if both are used in the same pattern.

### Fair Isle-type knitting

When two or three colors are worked repeatedly across a row, strand the yarn not in use loosely behind the stitches being worked. If you are working with more than two colors, treat the "floating" yarns as if they were one yarn and always spread the stitches to their correct width to keep them elastic. It is advisable not to carry the stranded or "floating" yarns over more than three stitches at a time, but to weave them under and over the color you are working. The "floating" yarns are therefore caught at the back of the work.

## Knitting ribs

All ribs should be knitted to a firm tension; for some knitters it may be necessary to use a smaller needle. In order to prevent sagging in cuffs and welts, it is best to use a "knitting-in" elastic.

# Finishing instructions

After knitting for hours making a garment, it seems a great pity that many garments are spoiled because little care is taken in the finishing process. These tips will give you a professional-looking garment.

## Pressing

Darn in all ends neatly along the selvage edge or a color join, as appropriate. Block out each piece of knitting using pins and gently press it, omitting the ribs, using a warm iron over a damp cloth.

**TIP:** Take special care to press the edges, as this will make sewing up both easier and neater.

## Stitching

When stitching the pieces together, remember to match areas of color and texture very carefully where they meet. Use a seam stitch such as backstitch or mattress stitch for main knitting seams and join all ribs and neckbands with a flat seam, unless otherwise stated.

## Construction

Having completed the pattern instructions, join left shoulder and neckband seams as detailed above.

Sew the top of the sleeve to the body of the garment using the method detailed in the pattern, referring to the appropriate guide:

### STRAIGHT BIND-OFF (CAST-OFF) SLEEVES

Place center of bound-off (cast-off) edge of sleeve to shoulder seam. Sew top of sleeve to body, using markers as guidelines where applicable.

### SET-IN SLEEVES

Set in sleeve, easing sleeve head into armhole.
Join side and sleeve seams.

### SQUARE SET-IN SLEEVES

Set sleeve head into armhole, the straight sides at top of sleeve to form a neat right-angle to bound-off (cast-off) sts at armhole on back and front.

### SHALLOW SET-IN SLEEVES

Join bound-off (cast-off) sts at beg of armhole shaping to bound-off (cast-off) sts at start of sleeve-head shaping. Sew sleeve head into armhole, easing in shaping.

Slipstitch pocket edgings and linings into place. Sew on buttons to correspond with buttonholes. After sewing up, press seams and hems. Ribbed welts and neckbands and any areas of garter stitch should not be pressed.

# abbreviations

| | |
|---|---|
| k | knit |
| p | purl |
| st(s) | stitch(es) |
| inc | increas(e)(ing) |
| dec | decreas (e) (ing) |
| st st | stockinette stitch (1 row k, 1 row p) |
| garter st | garter stitch (k every row) |
| beg | begin(ning) |
| foll | following |
| rem | remain(ing) |
| rev | revers(e) (ing) |
| rep | repeat |
| alt | alternate |
| cont | continue |
| patt | pattern |
| tog | together |
| mm | millimeters |
| cm | centimeters |
| in | inch(es) |
| RS | right side |
| WS | wrong side |
| Sl 1 | slip one stitch |
| psso | pass slipped stitch over |
| p2sso | pass 2 slipped stitches over |
| tbl | through back of loop |
| M1 | make one stitch by picking up horizontal loop before next stitch and knitting into back of it |
| yfwd | yarn forward |
| yrn | yarn around needle |
| yon | yarn over needle |
| cn | cable needle |

# conversions

## Needle sizes

Knitting needles are sized according to a standard sizing system, whatever material they are made from. There are three different systems: a metric system used in Europe and the UK; a US system; and an old UK and Canadian system.

| METRIC SIZE | US SIZE | OLD UK & CANADIAN SIZE |
|---|---|---|
| 10 | 15 | 000 |
| 9 | 13 | 00 |
| 8 | 11 | 0 |
| $7^1/_2$ | $10^1/_2$ | 1 |
| 7 | $10^1/_2$ | 2 |
| $6^1/_2$ | $10^1/_2$ | 3 |
| 6 | 10 | 4 |
| $5^1/_2$ | 9 | 5 |
| 5 | 8 | 6 |
| $4^1/_2$ | 7 | 7 |
| 4 | 6 | 8 |
| $3^1/_4$ | 5 | 9 |
| $3^1/_4$ | 4 | 10 |
| 3 | 2/3 | 11 |
| $2^3/_4$ | 2 | 12 |
| $2^1/_4$ | 1 | 13 |
| 2 | 0 | 14 |

## Converting weights and lengths

| | | |
|---|---|---|
| oz | = | g × 0.0352 |
| g | = | oz × 28.35 |
| in | = | cm × 0.3937 |
| cm | = | in × 2.54 |
| yds | = | m × 0.9144 |
| m | = | yds × 1.0936 |

# Embroidery stitches

### Blanket Stitch

Secure the thread at the edge of the knitting. Bring the thread out on the lower line, insert needle in position in the upper line, taking a straight downward stitch with the thread under the needle point. Pull up the stitch to form a loop. Repeat, leaving a small gap between the stitches. Continue along the edge, making all the stitches the same height.

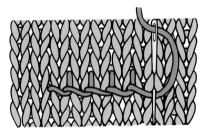

### French Knot

Bring the thread out at the required position. Wind yarn round twice or three times. Turn, pulling twists tightly against the needle, and insert it close to where it where the yarn first emerged. Pull yarn through to back.

### Stem Stitch

Bring the thread through, taking short stitches along the line as required. Continue making short, slightly angled overlapping stitches in this way from left to right.

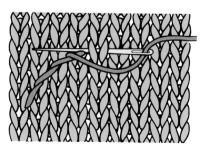

### Satin Stitch

Bring the thread through, then work stitches close together. Stitches can be made straight across or at an angle depending on the required finish. Care must be taken to keep a good edge; do not pull thread too tightly, or the knitting will be distorted.

### Lazy Daisy Stitch

Bring the thread through and hold down with left thumb. Thread through again where it last emerged, looping yarn under tip of needle, and fasten loop with small stitch. Make the required number of chains to form flower petals.

# Yarn information

### Rowan All-Seasons Cotton

60% cotton/40% acrylic/microfiber, approximately 90m (98yds) per 50g (1³/₄oz) ball

### Rowan Cotton Glacé

Lightweight cotton yarn 100% cotton, approximately 115m (125yds) per 50g (1³/₄oz) ball

### Rowan Fine Cotton Chenille

Lightweight chenille yarn 89% cotton/11% polyester, approximately

160m (175yds) per 50g (1³/₄oz) ball

**Rowan 4-ply Soft**

100% merino wool, approximately 175m (191yds) per 50g (1³/₄oz) ball

**Rowan Handknit DK Cotton**

Medium-weight cotton yarn 100% cotton, approximately 85m (92yds) per 50g (1³/₄oz) ball

**Rowan Kidsilk Haze**

70% super kid mohair 30% silk, approximately 210m (230yds) per 25g (00oz) ball

**Rowan Lurex Shimmer**

80% viscose 20% polyester yarn, approximately 95m (104yds) per 25g (00oz) ball

**Rowan Magpie Aran**

Aran-weight wool yarn 100% wool, approximately 140m (153yds) per 100g (3³/₄oz) hank

**Rowanspun DK**

100% pure new wool, approximately 200m (219yds) per 50g (3³/₄oz) ball

**Rowan True 4-ply Botany**

4-ply-weight yarn (US fingering) 100% pure new wool, approximately 170m (185yds) per 50g (1³/₄oz) ball

**Rowan Wool Cotton**

Double-knitting weight wool and cotton yarn (between US sport and worsted) 50% merino wool/50% cotton, approximately 113m (123yds) per 50g (1³/₄oz) ball

**Jaeger Extra Fine Merino DK**

A double-knitting-weight wool yarn; 100% extra fine merino wool; 125m (137yds) per 50g (1³/₄oz) ball

**Jaeger Luxury Tweed**

65% Merino lambswool 35% alpaca, 180m (197 yds) per ball

**Jaeger Matchmaker Merino Aran**

Aran-weight wool yarn 100% merino wool, approximately 82m (74yd) per 50g (1¾oz) ball.

**Jaeger Shetland Aran**

80% wool 20% alpaca, approximately 166m (182 yds) per 100g (3³/₄oz) ball

**Jaeger Cashmina**

80% cashmere 20% extra fine merino blend, approximately 125m (138yds) per 25g ball

# *how to measure your teddy*

Before starting to knit it is essential to measure your teddy and draw a diagram of the back, front and sleeve. Make a note of all the measurements.

The finished measurements of the garments vary according to style. Though actual measurements are included in the book, check measurements carefully as adjustments may have to be made to the body or sleeve length.

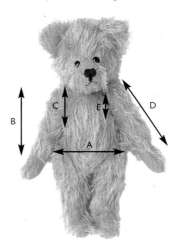

Width of back and front of body (**A**).

Length of body to shoulder (**B**).

Armhole depth (**C**).

Sleeve length (**D**).

Front neck depth (**E**).

Back neck width (**F**).